Responding to Student Expectations

OECD

ORGANISATION FOR ECONOMIC CO-OPERATION AND DEVELOPMENT

ORGANISATION FOR ECONOMIC CO-OPERATION AND DEVELOPMENT

Pursuant to Article 1 of the Convention signed in Paris on 14th December 1960, and which came into force on 30th September 1961, the Organisation for Economic Co-operation and Development (OECD) shall promote policies designed:

- to achieve the highest sustainable economic growth and employment and a rising standard of living in Member countries, while maintaining financial stability, and thus to contribute to the development of the world economy;
- to contribute to sound economic expansion in Member as well as non-member countries in the process of economic development; and
- to contribute to the expansion of world trade on a multilateral, non-discriminatory basis in accordance with international obligations.

The original Member countries of the OECD are Austria, Belgium, Canada, Denmark, France, Germany, Greece, Iceland, Ireland, Italy, Luxembourg, the Netherlands, Norway, Portugal, Spain, Sweden, Switzerland, Turkey, the United Kingdom and the United States. The following countries became Members subsequently through accession at the dates indicated hereafter: Japan (28th April 1964), Finland (28th January 1969), Australia (7th June 1971), New Zealand (29th May 1973), Mexico (18th May 1994), the Czech Republic (21st December 1995), Hungary (7th May 1996), Poland (22nd November 1996), Korea (12th December 1996) and the Slovak Republic (14th December 2000). The Commission of the European Communities takes part in the work of the OECD (Article 13 of the OECD Convention).

The Programme on Institutional Management in Higher Education (IMHE) started in 1969 as an activity of the OECD's newly established Centre for Educational Research and Innovation (CERI). In November 1972, the OECD Council decided that the Programme would operate as an independent decentralised project and authorised the Secretary-General to administer it. Responsibility for its supervision was assigned to a Directing Group of representatives of governments and institutions participating in the Programme. Since 1972, the Council has periodically extended this arrangement; the latest renewal now expires on 31st December 2006.

The main objectives of the Programme are as follows:

- to promote, through research, training and information exchange, greater professionalism in the management of institutions of higher education; and
- to facilitate a wider dissemination of practical management methods and approaches.

*
* *

Publié en français sous le titre :
Répondre aux attentes des étudiants

Foreword

As part of its 1999-2000 work programme, the OECD Programme on Institutional Management in Higher Education (IMHE) identified as a priority a project to provide institutions with a range of information on the management implications of changing student expectations. The impetus for this came, in part, from a series of reports, including the OECD's *Redefining Tertiary Education*, which highlighted the growing pressures on institutions to respond more effectively to an increasingly diverse and demanding student body, while in many cases simultaneously coping with increasing resource constraints. The project was managed by Professor Peter Coaldrake and Dr Lawrence Stedman, of the Queensland University of Technology, who also edited the papers in this publication.

Initially, the project was developed in an on-line format, using a Web page and e-mail discussion forum. Information about the project and the website address was emailed to over 200 individuals drawn from a listing of IMHE members and other contacts. The target group comprised students, academics and non-academic staff from European, UK and Australian universities. In the course of these discussions, the multiple dimensions of this issue became apparent, and in order to sharpen the focus of the project, particular issues were selected for consideration at two special seminars. Rather than examining specific instances of institutional management change, and highlighting what might be considered "best practice", it was decided that there would be more value in exploring more fundamental issues about the framework of relationships within which student expectations developed and affected universities.

The issues selected covered the nature of relationships among students, universities and other communities of interest; student and institutional perspectives on these relationships and their implications; and legal issues and public policy perspectives. The first of the seminars was held in Brisbane, Australia, on September 22 2001, and the second in Paris on 3-4 December 2001. The papers in this volume are an edited selection of those presented and discussed at those meetings.

The nature of student expectations and the form of appropriate university responses are clearly complex issues, touching on almost all aspects of higher education. Universities find themselves pushed on the one hand to respond to mounting expectations, while on the other there are fears that the fundamental purpose of higher education could be distorted or even lost if institutions go too far in the direction of placing university education on a quasi-commercial footing. Further, while many of the relevant issues have international resonance, being shared across different countries and systems of higher education, the responses of universities take place in particular national and local contexts. It is therefore inevitable that the following papers can only cover a small part of the relevant territory. Nevertheless there is considerable value in sharing experience, knowledge and reflections about these matters, not least to add some depth to a topic which is all too often discussed in sweeping and simplistic terms.

Contents

Institutional Responses to Changing Student Expectations: Project Overview

Peter Coaldrake

It is readily apparent to all those who work in higher education that students have high expectations of their universities, and that these expectations are of greater complexity and a different order to those which might have applied in past decades. Further, the impact of these expectations and the ways in which a university responds to and shapes them is increasingly important for the future welfare of the university.

Nor are students the only "stakeholders" who have an interest in universities. Higher education has for many years been a mass rather than an elite activity, and while this has raised the profile and importance of the various roles of universities, it has also raised expectations that they will not only to be responsive to the needs of individuals, the professions, governments and the wider community but also that they will be institutions of leadership, creativity and scholarship, embedded in society rather than operating as ivory towers. The contemporary university therefore faces major management challenges in working with multiple, often competing, demands and expectations including, prominently, those of its students.

It is possible to sketch some of the broad parameters of student expectations. They include, for example, expectations of quality and professionalism in the provision of university amenities and services; of access to suitably qualified teachers and learning support; of the value of programs of study to the student's later life, and their professional working life in particular; of convenience in the delivery of education; of being treated with respect; of value for money; and of high academic standards. As a general observation, more students are engaged in activities outside their chosen areas of study, particularly in paid employment, and expect universities to adapt the provision of higher education to accommodate these external demands on their time. In practical terms these expectations may manifest themselves in demand for "24/7" access to services, or equivalent access to staff, and in demand for a broadening in the nature of the interactions between students and universities and in particular in terms of the mix of physical and virtual environments for student learning. The concept of "telepresence" is assuming greater importance, so that students can now study at a physical campus, at home, or at work. Such developments demonstrate how technology has the potential to reshape our ideas about time and place in higher education, and is already blurring earlier distinctions between on-campus and distance education, or between on-shore and off-shore delivery.

However it is grossly misleading to imagine that these expectations apply in any uniform manner across the increasingly diverse body of students, even within a single university, much less globally.

As Richard James points out:

"Student preferences and expectations, and the relationships of these to institutional expectations and priorities, are exceedingly complex issues for analysis. The complexity is caused in the main part by the highly participatory nature of the higher education enterprise and the two-way interaction between the actions of students and those of universities – the higher education process not only shapes student expectations, the education process is itself influenced by the character of student expectations.

There is presently no single theoretical framework that adequately deals with these relationships."

The OECD/IMHE project on management responses to student expectations provided an opportunity to examine these complex issues in some depth. The papers in this volume were among those presented and discussed at two seminars in 2001, one in September held in Brisbane, Australia, the other in December in Paris. The contributors brought to bear perspectives from several different higher education systems, including those of Europe, the United Kingdom, Canada and Australia.

The Australian higher education system was a particularly prominent focus for this project. There are two points which should be made in this regard. First, the Australian system provides in many ways an ideal case study of potential management responses to student expectations, for reasons to be outlined shortly. Second, despite the many differences among national higher education systems in areas such as structure, governance and student experience, there are many common issues facing universities in different countries, and many similarities in the values and aspirations of academics and students around the world.

In relation to the suitability of Australian higher education as a test case, it is a relatively young system, with the first university established in the middle of the nineteenth century and with all but nine of the 37 public universities having been established after 1960. Many Australian universities have therefore been modelled on, and drawn practices and staffing from, other institutions around the world, notably but not exclusively those in the United Kingdom and the United States.

The last fifteen years have seen major changes in the ways in which Australian universities are financed and managed, beginning with the abolition of the binary system in 1988 and the introduction of the so-called Unified National System, whereby institutional profiles are negotiated annually with the Federal Government. Despite the appearance of central government planning, there were also moves afoot to shift the mode of financing from block grants to universities to a system where students paid an increasing share of the cost of tuition. This began with overseas students and some categories of non-research postgraduate students, and has accelerated over the past decade to see the majority of postgraduate coursework programs offered on a full-fee basis, with a loan scheme recently introduced for these students.

In the words of Mike Gallagher, "during the 1990s we have seen in the massified higher education sector a shift from 'responsiveness to national needs' as mediated through central planning, resource allocation and regulation (at a time of high university dependence on the state) to 'responsiveness to students' as mediating labour market needs through their preferences and choices (during a transition to increasing university self-reliance)." This shift has created an environment of competition among universities, and all Australian universities have developed professional marketing operations covering local and international activities. Australia as a whole has built an international reputation for being quite aggressive and relatively successful in international marketing and recruitment, particularly in the South-East Asian region. Thus Australia provides an instructive case study of the pressures being experienced by universities around the world, and in particular the pressure to respond more effectively to rising student expectations.

The discussions at the September and December seminars, and the papers in this volume, can be considered in the light of four broad questions:

- What is the nature and context of the relationships between students and universities?
- How and why are student expectations changing?
- To what extent should universities respond to student expectations?
- How should universities respond?

The nature and context of the relationships between students and universities

Ruth Dunkin provides an informative and useful conceptualisation of the these relationships within the context of a broader trilateral relationship between the university, society and the student. Here the emphasis is on the fluidity of relationships, their interconnectedness, and their evolution within specific national settings. These characteristics may be seen, for example, in the shift in emphasis placed by governments in several countries, including Australia and the

United Kingdom, on the individual benefits of higher education, particularly in securing professional employment. This may be contrasted with the continued high valuation of the social dimensions of university education seen in several European countries. For example, Eva Münsterova notes in her paper that the Czech Republic is engaged in a process of rebuilding national institutions following four decades of Soviet domination, students are seen as an essential national resource in this light. Nevertheless, she also notes that despite official policy valuing students, academic attitudes in many cases emphasise their subordinate position in the university community.

One significant consequence of viewing the issue of student expectations against a trilateral framework is that responsiveness to students will of necessity have consequences for the ways in which universities meet, or fail to meet, other expectations. This does not only mean that the role of universities as social institutions could be downplayed by treating students as customers or clients, it also means there is a danger in reducing university education to a simple transaction with a (possibly fee-paying) individual. The social aspects of higher education, the role of universities in bringing students into contact with various communities in the course of their learning, as well as the co-generational nature of learning, are of fundamental importance, a point also made strongly by John Seely Brown and Paul Duguid in their book *The Social Life of Information* (Harvard Business School Press, 2000).

The student leaders involved in the two seminars were unanimous and emphatic in expressing the view that students did not want to be viewed simply as customers and clients. In John Byron's words: "students expect to be taken on a journey that to a considerable degree they cannot imagine at the outset. They expect to have input during the journey, because this is the only way they can learn to be anything other than passengers. But they do not expect to call the shots, to be given only what it is that they have the experience to ask for, or to be regarded simply as revenue sources."

How and why are student expectations changing?

Changes in student expectations are often attributed to the rise of the "student as customer", have driven a change in view by many governments of higher education towards a greater attention to the individual benefits it confers, and a consequent move to require students to shoulder an increasing share of the cost of tuition. Undoubtedly this is a significant factor, anyone who has dealt with student complaints is familiar with students pointing out that they or their parents have paid significant sums of money, and expect high standards of service and quality in return. Further, this emphasis is heightened by competition among universities for the best students and government financing mechanisms which in several countries has been designed explicitly to increase the influence of student choice. Such a shift has two discernible effects. First it positions students more directly as partial purchasers of education services, with associated heightened demands and expectations as consumers. And second the financial pressures on students are reflected in growing numbers of undergraduate students, including those in first-year education, working part-time or even full-time. The term "disengagement" is frequently used to describe the resultant withdrawal of students from participation in on-campus activities. Further, many postgraduate students return to university for further study while continuing to work on a part-time or full-time basis: many of these students want convenience, with modularised curricula and flexible delivery, and many are not interested in remaining on campus for any longer than they consider necessary. Universities face considerable challenges in accommodating such a variety of expectations, while maintaining a commitment to quality.

Richard James outlines some relevant research findings from his own group and others about how these changes are perceived by academic staff in Australia. Many academics believe that a consumerist pattern of thinking is prevalent among students. They offer anecdotal reports of students wanting "quick, easy and cheap education", expecting to be spoon-fed in their learning and demanding explicit value for money. The student leaders at the two seminars were again of one view on this matter: to the extent that students behaved like quasi-consumers, this was more shaped by external factors than driven by an intrinsic desire on the part of students to be treated as customers. In particular, if higher education was presented as a quasi-commercial individualised transaction, then students would adjust their expectations accordingly.

However, the shift in some countries towards requiring students to pay more for their higher education cannot in itself account for the phenomenon of rising student expectations, as one Norwegian attendee at the Paris seminar observed, because even in Scandinavian countries where tuition remains fully subsidised through State grants to universities, student expectations of those universities are increasing. Dennis Farrington suggests that the role of students has shifted from "a subordinate role in the *studium generale* to one of a consumer of services", this shift raises expectations of entitlements to certain clearly defined rights as well as obligations, even if these are not based on a contractual footing or established through a commercial relationship. Indeed, he notes that the Anglo-American trend towards applying at least in part a contractual analogy is not recognised in all European countries, and that in some countries students' rights are instead founded solely on public law.

Richard James also notes that external market-related factors, such as vigorous marketing and highly competitive admissions processes, also play a role in forming student expectations, as do factors beyond the market. James singles out

11

for particular attention the importance of the early formative experiences of students on campus in shaping student expectations. The corollary of this is that universities should at least consider the possibility that part of the responsibility for the growing detachment of students lies within the sector itself and is related to the less personal and possibly less intensive environment that might be created as a consequence of growing class sizes.

The role of marketing in shaping student expectations is also raised by Sarah Davies, who argues that marketing in higher education is about achieving the objectives of the university by understanding what potential students need and want. However, this does not imply that students understand in advance what their educational needs are, nor does it imply that universities should change themselves to become what they perceive students might find attractive. Such change could well be counter to the objectives of the university. Yet there is a danger in overselling the perceived virtues of a university to prospective students. Many Australian universities trumpet their success in placing graduates into jobs, or providing flexible modes of study which fit with other priorities in students' lives. Others highlight the world-class research they provide and the promise that their students will be part of some sort of "cutting-edge" experience. If these promises are not met adequately, dissatisfaction and demotivation are likely to follow.

One other driver of change in student expectations is the growing presence of information technology. At my own university, Queensland University of Technology in Brisbane, we have seen an exponential growth in students accessing on-line services across the range of university activities, and an accompanying rise in demand and expectations that state-of-the-art facilities will be made available. Some students remain unenthusiastic about using IT facilities, but these folks are rapidly becoming a minority. The university faces a major challenge in coming years both in meeting the demands from students for more bandwidth and more applications, and also in managing the level of expectations about the levels of service that can realistically be provided. The balance between investing in virtual and physical infrastructure, between IT facilities and services and buildings and grounds, is becoming an increasingly important issue. It is also reflected in an increasingly robust debate internationally about "clicks and mortar" versus our traditional view of "bricks and mortar".

To what extent should universities respond to student expectations?

There were two key aspects to the discussions on this topic. The first concerned areas where universities could legitimately be expected to be responsive to student expectations, while the second concerned the potential dangers of going too far in this direction.

Michael Gallagher clearly sets out the trend in Australian government policy to develop market, or quasi-market, mechanisms in university financing which were intended to increase the responsiveness of universities to students. He cites a number of examples of such responsiveness which have already occurred, such as advances in curriculum design, more flexible provision of courses and combinations of courses, improvements in teaching and assessment practices, and a growing focus on learning outcomes such as the development of specified attributes or qualities in graduates. He also suggests that there is considerable room for further change to accommodate the new demands of a more diverse body of students, many of whom expect universities to provide education which suits their needs and preferences, rather than those of academics.

The role of students as consumers, highlighted by Dennis Farrington, underlines the importance for universities to respond with appropriate clarity and fairness in the ways in which students are treated. The experience of the Ombudsman in different countries has highlighted problems with lack of well-defined processes for handling student complaints, poor record-keeping and a general lack of professionalism in managing the rights of students. These are clearly matters where universities have an obligation to meet the expectations of students in their (partial) guise as consumers.

Richard James provides a useful perspective based on Herzberg's proposition that two sets of environmental factors affect people's satisfaction and motivation in relation to work. *Hygiene factors*, such as the quality of working spaces and amenities, are associated with the level of personal comfort in the workplace. If these are inadequate then workers may be dissatisfied, but if they are adequate that does not in itself generate strong satisfaction. On the other hand, *motivation factors* such as inspiring leadership and intellectual stimulation can, if present, lift motivation and achievement. If such motivation factors are not present, workers will not necessarily be dissatisfied, but they will be less personally motivated. Applying these to higher education, James suggests that provision of good facilities and services is a necessary but insufficient condition for high student satisfaction and motivation. Deeper satisfaction, and better education, will result from more stimulating and challenging experiences for students, which may well work counter to pre-existing student expectations.

Perhaps surprisingly, the student union leaders are also at pains to warn against undiscriminating responsiveness to student expectations. They are strongly of the view that student consultation in academic matters is important, and that the student body should be actively engaged as a participant in the university, but challenging curricula, rigour and substance should not be traded-off in the interests of improving student satisfaction.

13

How should universities respond?

There has been considerable attention devoted in recent times to the rapid growth of for-profit universities in the United States, several of which are characterised by the promise of convenience, efficient service, and delivery of standardised and vocationally-specialised curricula which can be delivered in modular form, often on-line. Frequently such organisations are held up as exemplars of responsiveness, and it has been claimed that conventional universities must react to them as aggressive competitors, and improve their own efficiency and convenience, or else face obsolescence (Cunningham et al., 2000). Certainly the factors of efficiency and convenience are important, and the success of a small but significant minority of the for-profit institutions in the United States suggests that these matters are particularly highly valued by certain groups of students. However a clear message from the papers in this volume is that these factors are but two among many which must be addressed and balanced by universities.

While the two seminars repeatedly emphasised complexity and context when discussing university responses to student expectations, some specific suggestions for university management did emerge. One was the overall need to ensure greater transparency, meaning that clearly understood and accessible information should be provided to students about matters such as complaints processes and policies, availability of services, and various aspects of the educational experience. The latter amounts to a more formal codification of the respective roles and responsibilities of universities and students, as well as more detailed information about potential learning outcomes, assessment processes and curriculum structures. Such transparency can not only reduce student dissatisfaction by closing the gap between expectations and reality; it can also head off potential legal problems or external complaints. While there have been relatively few cases of students suing universities, the liability of universities is highlighted by the trends towards higher levels of fee-paying and marketing of higher education as a product. In the Australian situation, liability could be based not only on the general legal doctrine of negligence, but also on the fair trading provisions of the national *Trade Practices Act* 1974 and the equivalent State Fair Trading Acts. In many cases, as Anthony Moore points out, a fair trading claim would be likely to be joined with a negligence claim.

Another suggestion was for universities to take a more strategic approach to the management of student expectations, particularly in the light of evidence suggesting that such expectations are shaped significantly by the early experiences of first-year students. This management might take the form of more intensive work with students in the first few weeks of their course (going beyond the traditional university orientation activities), including advice on managing their time among their various commitments, and clarifying the nature and extent of support and facilities that are likely to be available to students throughout their studies. This may be particularly important where significant changes or innovations are made to teaching practices. There have been examples in the past where pedagogically sound changes to teaching and assessment have run into trouble because inadequate attention has been paid to the preparation of students and the conflict with their expectations of conventional lectures and tutorials. In such situations, students can feel that they are "guinea pigs" and will resist change, even if it is in their best educational interests.

More broadly, Richard James argues for a rethinking of the undergraduate curriculum. While well aware of the many existing pressures on the curriculum, he suggests that many universities have responded to these pressures in an incremental and piecemeal fashion. His suggestion is for a more holistic review of undergraduate education, which seeks to balance the realities of new forms of student interaction with the university against the need to ensure rigorous educational underpinnings and coherence of the curriculum.

Concluding comments

Given the many layers of complexity involved in the consideration of student expectations, it is inevitable that this project would only be able to touch on a relatively small selection of the relevant issues. It certainly was not in a position to develop "recipes" for institutional management action, or even point to what might be considered as best practice. There is clearly a wealth of knowledge yet to be developed about how student expectations are developed, how they evolve during the student's experience of university study, and how universities might best manage the potential friction between those expectations and the realities of institutional life.

For example, this project has not explored in any detail issues such as:

- Partnerships and alliances, and how these might assist in meeting student expectations.

- Technology both as a potential problem, given high expectations, and a potential solution.

- Generational influences, notably the claim in marketing research about differences in characteristics and expectations of "Generation Y" and "Generation X" (Wolburg and Pokrywczynski, 2001). These might underlie, for example, differences in student expectations about their ability to browse subjects, and make frequent changes in enrolment, a phenomenon which is causing increasing administrative headaches for some universities.

15

- The nature of student decision making, including the role of various actors such as career guidance counsellors, peers or family in mediating university marketing messages and enrolment decisions.

The nature of this project should therefore be understood to be one of early exploration, offering some clearer perspectives on issues which are frequently dealt with in an oversimplified manner.

Reference was made earlier to the differences as well as the similarities between the Australian situation and that pertaining elsewhere. In this regard it is interesting to compare the observations made at the Brisbane and Paris seminars with those made by Professor Richard J. Light, of the Graduate School of Education at Harvard University, in his recent and widely acclaimed book *Making the Most of College: Students Speak Their Minds*. In this book, Light reported on his findings from thirty years in higher education and the results of ten years of surveying Harvard seniors on their educational experience. While the US higher education scene differs significantly from that in Australia, for example, in the structural diversity of education providers, the tradition of on-campus residence, and the prominence of racial diversity as a contentious issue, many of the findings and recommendations are familiar. In particular, he highlights the need to improve the relevance and "fit" of higher education to the wider lives of students. He cites one dean as saying that his job was simply to recruit the best students and get out of their way. Light argues strongly that colleges and universities should not just get out of the way, and indeed that it should be an obligation of institutions of higher education to provide challenging experiences for students which engage them in the life of the university and the wider world, and which stretch their expectations. He further highlighted the importance of engaging with students in the first few weeks of the academic year. Undoubtedly it would be easier to achieve these sorts of changes if we all had the resources of Harvard University, but few of the examples Light uses involve a massive commitment of resources. More fundamentally they involve a commitment to the notion of student-centred learning. This has become something of a catch-phrase which is easily misinterpreted as treating students like clients or customers. Rather, it should mean treating student learning as a clear goal of university education, and structuring it accordingly, making it the business of the university to understand student needs and to respond appropriately, and treating students with the respect they deserve and demand.

References

CUNNINGHAM, S., RYAN, Y., STEDMAN, L., TAPSALL, S., BAGDON, K., FLEW, T. and COALDRAKE, P. (2000),
The Business of Borderless Education, Evaluations and Investigations Program, 00/3 July, Department of Education, Training and Youth Affairs, Canberra.

LIGHT, R.J. (2001),
Making the Most of College: Students Speak Their Minds, Harvard University Press.

WOLBURG, J.M. and POKRYWCZYNSKI, J. (2001),
"A psychographic analysis of Generation Y college students", *Journal of Advertising Research*, 41(5), pp. 33-52.

Higher Education, Students, Society: Multi-lateral Relationships

Ruth Dunkin

Introduction

Although the concept of students as customers of universities now has widespread acceptance, its use simplifies the nature of the relationship. It tends also to suggest that the relationship is private, but the existence of significant public subsidies deny this. Public universities are accountable for student outcomes not only to students, but also to government funding bodies, employers, and the broader community. These accountabilities are not separate; they are intermeshed. How do we understand these?

This chapter explores the complexity of the relationship between the university and student and puts it within the context of a broader trilateral relationship between the university, society and the student. The relationship between university and student alone can be seen as incorporating both transactional and process elements, paralleling the provision of professional services in other sectors. Students need to be seen as people with many different roles within society that must be acknowledged in the formation of the relationship. But while important, the relationship between university and student must be balanced by university managers, with obligations to and the expectations of the community in the conduct of its work. Further, students themselves seek to, and have, obligations to and with the community.

This chapter also recognizes that the trilateral relationship and the different expectations and conceptions of roles of each of the parties vary between countries, shaped by the national policy and cultural settings in which it occurs. The roles of each party become self-reinforcing and mutually influencing and often have more in common with each other than with their counterparts in different settings. This chapter is written from an Australian perspective.

The relationship between the university, student and society

Duderstadt (2001) has talked of the transition in the United States from student to learner to consumer. In this he reflects upon the impact of deregulation and market forces upon the changing dynamics of the education sector, the characteristics of its demand and supply. Sister Read of Alverno, too, suggests that "students have begun acting like customers and the student watchword for education has become 'quick, easy and cheap'... the degree is presented primarily if not exclusively as an economic advantage" (2001, p. 87).

Those of us in Anglo-American countries would recognize the truth in these descriptions. Yet even for us, does this redefinition of the relationship between student and university capture the totality of the relationship? Should it? A customer relationship, based on the model of private sector transactions, is a limited and voluntary exchange, from which the customer derives a private value. Despite introducing in many Anglo-American countries a customer focus to public sector services as a means of improving their effectiveness, the concept of customer exchange does not easily extend to all areas of public sector activity. For example, prisoners are not "customers" of prisons – there is little perceived private value – and a taxpayer's obligation to pay tax is not conceived as voluntary. In some public sector transactions, then, a person may be positioned as a citizen or obligatee rather than a consumer.

Using social exchange theory, Alford's (2002) model of interaction between different agents in the provision of public services provides a way of understanding the reciprocities involved. These have particular import in the context of a knowledge-based economy.

- *University – student*. Student receives educational services, and in most cases in Australia today, pays some money directly to the institution for the program, although the total cost may be subsidized. The amount paid by students is set by Government taking account of differential future earnings (or private value) by profession. In the case of full-fee programs or employers buying training for their employees, the exchange between the University and student has been framed as a private exchange.

- *Student – community*. The student provides skills and knowledge back into the community to underpin the social and economic development of that community. In some cases, there is a specific obligation accepted by the student in return for their education – for example, those medical students who have accepted that they will practice in rural areas upon graduation. There is also a social positioning function of education, with the student being rewarded personally through social status and remuneration.

- *Community – university*. The community provides resources via taxation to support education and research, and in return receives public goods of increased knowledge and educated population, together with a contribution to the development of social capital.

Although this schema provides a way of conceiving the trilateral relationship, its reality is not static. Changes in our society and economy lead to consequential variations in the character of these relationships and the expectations underpinning them. The nature of these will be outlined in more detail in the following sections, but include the growing significance of learning to learn as an attribute; the implications of the diversity of students in determining what are their expectations, including the significance of student-as-worker, and the emerging understanding by the community and employers of what constitutes knowledge.

Nor are these relationships mutually exclusive. The strong (but not exclusive) influence of the family, for example, has been well documented in guiding student choice, expectations and behavior. To the extent that they are often a source of financial support (Birrell *et al.*, 2000) parents too have expectations of what is or should be provided that do not necessarily mirror those of the students themselves, governments or employers. A significant shaper of their expectations, in turn, is their own experience. Not only are the boundaries dissolving between different spheres of activity (work education, personal), but also we are increasingly recognizing that the multiple roles people play cannot be cleanly separated.

Figure 1. **The trilateral relationship between student, community and university**
National culture and prevailing political/economic/social philosophy

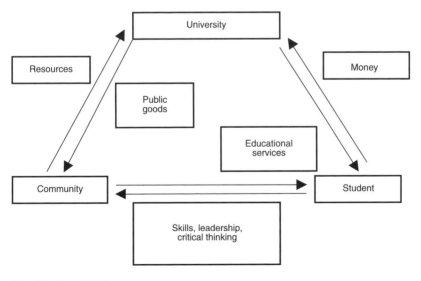

Source: Based on Alford (2002).

This model is set within specific national policy settings. The cultural norms implicit within these shape views about the role and value of tertiary education and thus expectations of each of the parties. For example, in some countries, such as the Czech Republic (Münsterova, 2002), governments see universities as major vehicles for embedding democratic thinking and practice. In this case the student-as-citizen is the prevailing role articulation for students. By contrast, despite the argument in this chapter for a broader conception of student, the underlying legal representation of students in Anglo/American societies is as "consumers" (Farrington, 2001).

Who are our students?

Participation in higher education has increased significantly in most OECD countries over the past 15 years, arising from expanded access to school-leavers and to a growing trend to continuing professional development. This has led to greater diversity among students in terms of age, social and educational back-ground, engagement in work, family status and ethnicity. This has been accelerated too by the increase in international education. For example, in 2000 international students represented 12.6% of those studying in Australian universities.

In the past 20 years, the levels of study have been strongly related to particular points in the career/life cycle. There are three main groups of students studying in our institutions. The first and generally the largest comprises undergraduate students. In the past two decades in Australia these were full-time school leavers, with study a "time out" interregnum between two major life stages, and involving a significant socialization process. However, today fewer Australian students experience a linear progression from school to tertiary study to work. Entry to the workforce is increasingly interwoven with study for both school leavers and the mature student.

The second group is post-graduate coursework students. Typically these are adults in work returning to study to advance or change their existing careers. In Australia, as in many other countries, there has been a significant increase in post-graduate coursework and continuing professional development programs aimed at these people. Many of these are supplied by non-traditional educational pro-viders attracted by the increased demand for continuing skill upgrades and better able to "deliver" in a "just in time", time efficient and convenient manner. Postgraduate coursework programs represent about 10% of the total provision of Australian universities, and while the volume of non-credit continuing profes-sional development is difficult to measure, it is clearly growing.

The third group, representing about 5% of the total, are the research students. They occupy a different intermediate space between students and academics, apprentices and practitioners. Again this group has grown over the past decade and has similarly diversified. Research-based education is pursued not only by young adults who would seek to become academics or researchers, but also by mature adults in other sectors who seek both to improve their own current practice and add to the body of knowledge for that practice.

Underpinning these changes to the student body during the past decade are three major themes. First there is a clear recognition by students and their families that education is critical to individual career and thus social and economic success. For international students this has meant access to Western education. Second, by expanding access and the numbers engaged in higher education governments have sought to ensure that these private benefits were available widely. Third, governments have also understood the importance for economic development of an educated and skilled workforce and the potential of education as an export industry.

In Australia, policy reforms successfully expanded provision from 450 000 students in 1991 to 529 000 in 1998, increasing participation by school leavers from 34% in 1993 to 47% in 1999. At the same time the proportion of the population with higher degrees rose from 10% to 14%. This expansion of access led to a corresponding broadening of the student population and a greater diversity in backgrounds, expectations and preparation. The changing nature of employment, the reintroduction of fees (both partial and full) and the impact of widespread access to digital technologies have also led to a change in the manner of engagement by Australian undergraduate students (McInnis, 2001) and changed expectations of their learning experiences. The implications of these will be dealt with below.

The relationship between the university and student

The relationship between student and institution can be seen in two interconnected parts. The first relates to the administrative and academic transactions between student and institution and the second to the educational process itself. While the consumerist ethos has and should influence the first, good quality service in these transactions is insufficient to assure a good student experience.

Expectations of service

The student's interaction with the university is made up of a series of small transactions – borrowing library books, seeking course information, enrolling – in which timeliness, responsiveness and a client service ethos are very important.[1] The deficiencies of university systems largely built in a period when students' time was assumed to be cheap are an ongoing concern for students. This is particularly so for part-time postgraduate students with family and work commitments and whose expectations of what constitutes appropriate service are set within their own workplaces at increasingly higher levels. They are no longer content to attend physically when web or telephone transactions could substitute; they are no longer content to await assessment results until a time that accommodates the academic's other priorities. They expect information about programs and fees to be readily available and accurate.

The service ethos expectation also spills over into what may be seen as academic matters – the programming and sequencing of the program itself. Timetables, student/staff interactions and even learning experiences have been designed for the majority of students as if they are available on-campus full-time. Indeed, the past decade had seen a shift in undergraduate student bodies from part-time students studying on campus at night to predominantly full-time students. Most recent surveys, however (McInnis, 2001), have seen Australian undergraduates once again juggling work and study but now within a labor market in which casualisation and more flexible labor practices have resulted in a different timing of work. Night classes on campus are now often insufficient to accommodate these schedules. On the other hand, many international undergraduates and a significant minority of Australian undergraduates continue to want a daytime campus-based experience not consistent with the needs of others. This has implications for flexibility and choice in the mode of engagement by students with the university and presents some significant challenges in the design of the educational curriculum itself. For example, as a means of preparing people to work in an increasingly diverse and globalizes workplace, educators seek study abroad elements within programs. How can the same learning outcomes be achieved if students are constrained in their study by work and place commitments?

The educational process

What is "education"?

Students come to us for education and training. In some cases this is for specific skills and knowledge; in others, it is to develop broader capabilities and personal attributes, including acquiring a specific body of knowledge. It involves developing new understandings and news ways of seeing phenomena (Bowden and Marton, 1998). It is not merely a process of acquiring new facts or information, even though this might be the expectation of incoming students (Coaldrake and Stedman, 2001). The role of the academic or teacher is to facilitate the development of these new ways of seeing through designing a series of learning experiences that inform, provoke and challenge the student's ways of understanding the particular phenomenon. The role of the student is to engage actively with the process, undertaking those tasks required, participating in the experiences. It is an interactive process, a process of co-generation of learning outcomes.

The nature of the relationship

To illustrate, the relationship of the individual student to the university can be likened to that of a client seeking professional services like accounting or health care. As with signing up to a course of medical treatment, the agreement between student and institution is not simply an exchange of money for services. The patient is trusting the doctor's experience in treating other patients, and must submit to her judgement, while at the same time being an active participant in the treatment – undertaking exercises, taking prescribed medication, monitoring her own condition. Although moves by regulatory bodies have sought to increase the information in the hands of the "consumer", there is a limit to the information available and informed judgements that can be made by the recipient of the service. There is therefore an incipient imbalance in the power between academic and student.

Making the obligations more explicit

The recent moves towards learner-centered teaching and learning within universities recognize first that learning, the ultimate outcome desired of the process of education, does not occur unless the learner participates in the process, and importantly, *wants* to learn. Second, they recognize that even when learners do have a desire to learn, their individual learning styles differ. Bowden and Marton (1998) have identified variation as a key source of learning, suggesting that the same concept will be the subject of deep learning, the desired outcome, when approached in different ways. Yet many learners, particularly at the undergraduate level, are not sufficiently aware of their own learning styles nor familiar with the range of educational process interventions available to support or trigger learning. Rather their expectations of how learning occurs and what is "education" are formed by their previous experience. Academic staff have anecdotal and sometimes survey data from past alumni showing how students' perceptions of the relevance and power of particular learning experiences change some years after graduation. Moreover, an implication of the diversity of the student body is that no simple assumptions can be made about students' prior experiences or the expectations that flow from them. Not only is there significant variation in the way in which Australian schools educate students, but also the educational models, processes and cultures used in those countries from which we recruit international students vary significantly.

Efforts to improve student success and to reduce the gap in expectations are evidenced by the move by most institutions to introduce transition to (tertiary) study programs and develop "learning contracts". The former seek to ensure that entering undergraduate students have the basic literacies and skills to undertake their programs. They also help establish expectations of the respective roles of academic and student at the undergraduate level. While these programs appear to have contributed to reducing the high attrition rates in first year, further work is required to have students explore their own learning style and for academics to articulate learning outcomes and the rationale of the learning design. This is particularly so for international students who seek an Australian educational experience but often have little conception of what that entails.

The concept of the partnership between students and staff to reach an agreed goal has been embodied by many institutions in the form of a "learning contract", making explicit the responsibilities of each party. This contract asks students to take responsibility for their own learning. Its success depends on students' ability to articulate their desired goals. The parallel responsibility of the institution is to empower students to be able to fulfil this responsibility. For many the notion of education as a more balanced partnership entailing mutual obligations appears a radical departure from the concept of education as the imparting of knowledge from the "master" to the student, where the obligations respectively are to give and to receive. But the concept is not new. Socrates in meeting with his students asked them to think, to develop by logic a deeper understanding and awareness of the various phenomena under study. He facilitated and guided their learning and development.

Role of mutual engagement: students

Engagement and enthusiasm by both parties has long been seen as critical to successful learning (Pascarella and Terenzini, 1998) but a common perception of academics is that many undergraduate students are increasingly disengaged and lack the commitment required for successful education (McInnis, 2001). This perception arises, McInnis notes, from the declining numbers in classrooms and from the requests for special arrangements to meet the demands of paid work.

> "The range of institutions, courses and subjects now available, combined with the increasingly sophisticated access to flexible modes of knowledge delivery and electronically generated communities of learners, puts students in a powerful position to shape the undergraduate experience to suit their own timetables and priorities" (2001, p. 3).

McInnis believes that to interpret these actions as "disengagement" is to imply a deficit in attitudes on the part of students and to misjudge their intentions. This can only lead to a misunderstanding of their expectations and realities and an inappropriate response by institutions. He argues that the pattern of engagement between student and institution must be renegotiated and this will be within dimensions of the curriculum (sequence and patterning), new patterns of creating learning communities and issues of infrastructure and support for the total student experience. To do this we need to recognize that students' styles of learning are changing from those with which we are familiar. They are no longer linear either in building knowledge or in accessing theory before application. Duderstadt (2001) describes those who have been raised in a media-rich environment: they learn through experimentation and participation; they learn through collaboration and interaction; their thinking is non-linear and characterized by parallel processing. Education becomes "just-in-time".

Coaldrake (2000) talks of a future where universities move from being a reality that is constructed and controlled by academics to one as experienced by students. By re-engaging with students as people with multiple roles, we recognize the variety of experiences they bring to the educational process. Increasingly as they intermesh periods of employment and study, we have the opportunity to help them make sense of the experiences and the data they have from these other roles by providing them with conceptual and analytical frameworks.

Some misunderstand the nature of the change and as a result seek to frame a debate around whether we should give students what they want or what is "good" for them.

These are valid points but this is not the same issue as one that requires us to grapple with the changing characteristics and needs of our students, and with these our relationship with them. The implications of striving for a more productive balance place a responsibility on staff to acknowledge the power differential between themselves and students and work in a way that reduces this gap, to transform the relationship into a partnered approach, reflecting the way in which many social and economic relationships within the knowledge economy are being reconfigured.

At the same time, if our role is to prepare people for an uncertain future (Bowden and Marton, 1998), then students need to accept judgements that they must take responsibility for their own learning. To cope with such a future they will need effective self-management and ongoing learning capabilities if they are to prosper and thrive, even survive, in an environment of continuous change. In increasingly complex working environments and a climate of unstable employment, the skills of self-management have become key for all professions. Many universities have recognized this importance and articulated it in statements of graduate capabilities.

Role of mutual obligations: ours

So what is our obligation? James' research (2001) with undergraduate students has led him to believe students' motivations and desires have not changed much in the past 20 years. They have always balanced liberal educational aims with instrumentalism. Students themselves exhort us to maintain academic rigor, to pursue content and experiences we believe are important even in the face of their unpopularity with students.[2]

Reservations from academic staff about the pre-eminence granted to student evaluations of teaching quality reside in uneasiness about the extent to which students can make informed judgements about the totality of their experiences. Others (Correa, 2001) believe that grade inflation is a direct result of the use of student evaluations of faculty. Some student leaders agree. Their voices sum their expectations of us:

> "Students expect to be taken on a journey that – they cannot imagine at the outset. They expect to have input during the journey …" (Byron, 2002).

> "Students' expectations are formulated in the context of what universities hold out they are offering. If universities are offering credentialing, then students will demand 'quick, easy and cheap'…" (Henderson, 2001).

Staff all understand and accept their professional responsibilities to keep up to date in their own fields. However as the knowledge sector becomes more diverse and demand grows for recognition of others' contributions to generating and disseminating knowledge, new obligations are emerging. First in relation to teaching staff, there is a need to strengthen understanding of educational theory and best practice. As we are called upon to accredit educational experiences gained elsewhere, perhaps within different pedagogies, we must understand their relationship to those we use. As the diversity of our students grows we need to understand the new and different ways in which people learn and how new techniques or types of learning experiences can facilitate that learning. Second, we need to create new conceptual frameworks that acknowledge and locate the different sorts of knowledge in use (Barnett, 2000).

Indeed we need to role model the continuous learner we encourage our students to become. We are not immune to the forces that generate the need for continuous learning.

Empowering students to participate equally in the process of education will always be a contested area. Although culturally many of us seek to separate the professional from the personal, as the multiple roles and experiences of students are recognized, the boundary between work, study and recreation is blurring. This raises questions about appropriate approaches to student support and the provision of "pastoral care", particularly as these can be a key element in helping students "put the pieces together". By recognizing that the difficulties arising in aspects of their life outside study – relationships, housing, finance and health – can impact severely a student's capacity to achieve success, these services become integral to learning support, in the same way as are additional tutorial, specific academic skills and information resource access. Rather than being an add-on or a safety net, these services can connect with key learning outcomes. If the central organizing outcome is each learner's success, then ensuring the right configuration of programmatic, learning support and administrative services for each student is critical.

In summary, then, the learning process itself involves a process of "co-generation" between learner and institution. However, that learner comes in the form of a person who has distinctive characteristics and often undertakes multiple roles. These often affect significantly the manner, timeliness and the scope of their preferences for learning as much as their individual learning styles and the rich experiential data that needs to be synthesized within conceptual frameworks. The growing level of user pays at each level of post-secondary education, combined with a new imperative around continuous learning and skill upgrading for careers, has led to a new consumerism within Australian higher education that is transforming the ways in which universities configure their academic and administrative operations. Just because the education process is one of co-generation does not mean there is no place for customer service in universities. Indeed, the very success of the non-traditional providers on this dimension alone has been sufficient to dislodge universities' claim to market monopoly. The very richness of diversity that now exists among our students is also our most significant challenge – to design cost-effective and appropriate learning experiences and learning support to meet the diverse needs of the people who are our students. As Duderstadt (2001) says: from "just-in-case" to "just-in-time" and now "just-for-you" education.

While primarily focusing on the engagement of the student with the educational process, there is also evidence of a decline in engagement with the life of the university more broadly. This has implications again for the changing role conception of "student". The capacity or preparedness of students to engage with the decision-making and extracurricular activities of the campus is lessening everywhere. Only 10-20% of students vote in key elections and fewer participate in club and on-campus activities. Although the notion of student-as-citizen arises in Australia (although not as strongly as in Europe), these trends point to changing patterns of engagement with the university community.

The relationship between student and community

As mentioned earlier, in some cases the community states its expectation of the graduate specifically – providing services in rural or remote areas, teaching for a number of years, serving in the defense forces for a number of years. Usually though the expectation of the community is expressed more diffusely. A general expectation prior to the "massification" of the system was that the educated elites would provide the future community and professional leadership for their communities. Now it is perhaps no more than being part of the general economic leadership and engine for growth. Yet the existence of public subsidies in most countries implies some public benefit from individual education.

From the students' perspective, however, a widespread view that theirs has been primarily an economic and private value transaction is changing. Focus groups on campus and the evolution of different type of student activities, often linked to the academic program, are heralding a greater desire to "make a difference". This can be linked to these trends more broadly within many societies.

The relationships between the university and society

Most universities in the past hundred years have met a combination of expectations of their community. Although it is fashionable in some quarters to portray the economic role of universities as part of a relatively recent move to utilitarianism, for most it has always been part of the role. For example, the education and training of the professions has long been part of many traditional universities and the US land grant universities have explicitly had a charter for economic development and support of particular industries. However in addition to these economic roles universities have been seen also to play a role in the maintenance and enhancement of the social and cultural development of their communities. Newman (2000) identifies three major roles traditionally performed by public universities. For undergraduate students they have played a socializing role, providing continuity and stability in cultures. They have also provided pathways to social mobility. Third, they have represented places of scholarly reflection and learning, where knowledge has been advanced and understanding and interpretation of the change around them have taken place.

Yet as we enter the new century there is no doubt that many within our communities are seeking a significant reorientation of role for universities. The imperative to find sustainable economic growth for all at a time of massive economic restructuring as a result of globalization of markets and new technologies is leading many to require a more outcome-focused economic contribution from universities. This takes the form of demands for graduates with skills more closely aligned with the needs of existing and future industries and enterprise development and for research and development that can be translated quickly into commercial applications.

These demands come too at a time when the structure of knowledge production itself is in significant change. It has become commonplace to note that universities have lost their traditional monopolies on knowledge-related activities. There are two major consequences. First, the sector, or industry, is increasingly subject to the same pressures for specialization that apply to other sectors as a means of meeting the cost and quality levels introduced by new competitors. Secondly, the loss of monopolies is accompanied by a redefinition of what constitutes knowledge itself (Gibbons, 1998). Both governments and employers are demanding that universities acknowledge broader definitions of knowledge and reflect this within university education. For example, they demand both "intellectual knowledge" and "experience-based knowledge" (Walshok, 1995). Yet at the same time they insist that we maintain academic rigor. In order to meet these apparently conflicting demands we must build the new conceptual knowledge frameworks. As Barnett states:

> The world calls for challenges to our frameworks by being offered new frameworks; and a responsibility falls upon the university to make its contribution to that requirement (2000, p. 120).

These changes have been driven by the necessity and demand for knowledge and information and have been facilitated by an increasingly well-educated workforce and widely available information. As the basis of competitive advantage and performance in organization changes from efficiency to innovation, application and specialization of knowledge, employers seek both specialized knowledge and personal attributes that allow that knowledge to be deployed within cross-functional teams and communicated to those outside the specialization. They seek therefore graduates who can demonstrate creativity, leadership, initiative, responsibility, teamwork and most importantly, a capacity and desire to continue to learn. For those organizations that seek to build sustainable advantage, continuing workplace learning is seen as essential (Sommerlad and Stern, 1998).

Sources of tension

There are currently two sources of conflict that universities must resolve in the trilateral relationship between student, university and community. The first relates to the content of the learning experience. If the question of "do we give students what they want or what (we perceive) is good for them?" applies to the relationship between university and student, a parallel question exists between university and community – "who knows best what is best for the student?" We can agree that the future we face is uncertain but we have varying views how best to prepare students to face it. The past record of both universities and employers would suggest that neither group has always predicted it correctly. Universities might tend to suggest that the most important attributes we can instill are learning to learn and understanding of underpinning concepts; employers might specify more immediate knowledge and attributes. However there are also questions about the most effective site and modes of learning. For example, there are those within organizations – for example Arie de Geus, the former head of education and training for Shell – who have observed that through structuring the learning experientially learning can occur more quickly than academics suggest possible. This returns us to the issue raised in the previous section – the need for us to be confident and professional in our understanding of educational theory and practice.

The other point of tension within this trilateral relationship relates to the extent to which new technologies will be used in the delivery of education. Governments and employers, anxious to maximize access and contain cost see the potential of new technologies to improve the efficiency with which education is "delivered". Employers are able to specify to institution and learners respectively the manner in which the training they purchase directly will be delivered and their learning will occur. A similar desire by many governments however is made more difficult by the indirect relationship they have with students. At present students themselves, particularly at the undergraduate level who can currently afford access, are highly skeptical about the use of more self-directed and electronically based education. They are happy to see it as an alternative giving them choice, but are far less happy to see it as the only manner of engagement with the institution. The feedback from current campus-based students, whether international or Australian, is that they want face-to-face interaction. For institutions, the question then becomes which stakeholder, or client, takes primacy. In a purely private market this tension would be resolved. In a hybrid market in which the learners are only partially paying, the institution is left to resolve the tensions.

Other roles of universities

There are some who believe that the non-economic roles of universities in relation to graduates are also important. Drucker (1999) talks of the new pluralism in our society, arising from specialization. He suggests that without leaders who manage beyond the boundaries of their organizations and in the face of the inevitable decline of our generalist social institutions that provided the glue of our society, society as community is threatened. These fears are echoed by others. For example, Putnam (1993) suggests that there has been an erosion of the social capital necessary to take effective collective action. He believes that while the market mechanism has been effective in maximizing many outcomes, it is ineffectual in dealing with some that have the nature of public goods, such as urban safety. Yet its existence in pockets, such as Silicon Valley and parts of Northern Italy have underpinned and been integral to new economic and social development. Burton-Jones (1999) too, claims that widespread anxieties about the future exist because of the radical restructuring of our societies and economies. He calls for closer examination of the contribution that universities can play in providing linkages, building communities of practice and enhancing social cohesion. The traditional roles of public universities will not be assumed by many of the new players. Newman (2000) has found that while those in the for-profit education market believe such roles are important, they do not believe that it is within their business mission to assume such roles. Yet they are integral to the formation of the social capital believed necessary to underpin the knowledge economy and the networked specialized enterprises that will populate it.

Finally, the relationship between the institution and the community moves beyond that which relates directly to students. The emerging demands for universities to be more outcome-focused in relation to their research and development activities recognizes the contribution expected of universities to local and national development. While this is seen as critical by industry and trade portfolios of government, it is often forgotten when considering the restructuring of expectations of universities in relation to their undergraduate teaching. Many universities, however, are seeking to articulate and enhance the potential cross-over in both activities for students and staff by adopting the Boyer scholarship model as a means of underpinning both research and development and teaching and learning.

Conclusion

There has been over recent years a preoccupation with redefining the student as customer. This has led to some much-needed improvements in the orientation of public universities to their students. These improvements need to continue. For example, the growing diversity of our students means that both programs and learning infrastructures need to be carefully retailored. Their increasing direct contribution to our revenues means that we cannot ignore our students' changing needs or demands for improved transactional service. In particular, there is an urgent need to re-consider the basis on which students seek to engage with their study and the competing demands for their time as they juggle work and family commitments. At least for many Australian students traditional linear patterns of study and work have been abandoned.

However reduction of the student-university relationship to one of customer and provider simplifies the relationship. A vexed question remains around the extent to which students themselves can dictate the way in which they engage with learning and access knowledge. The limits on their understanding of how and what they should learn are matched sometimes by similar limits within our institutions. The process of learning is an interactive process of co-generation involving both student and academic, with judgements to be made by both about the form of that process. But they are not the only ones who seek to judge these matters. Increasingly employers, with the support of governments concerned to ensure economic prosperity, are challenging universities' monopoly to determine alone what is taught. Yet universities' validation and accreditation of the development and acquisition of knowledge remains an important element within the education system. The recent concerns about "soft marking" and lowered standards are testimony that what people seek is flexible, responsive but still of "high quality". While there is growing skepticism about universities' judgements by many groups, to many others including the students themselves those judgements retain an intangible value because of the perceived independence of universities.

Reduction of the student-institution relationship to that of customer-provider also focuses attention on the benefits to the individual. This focus downplays the benefits of education to the community, diminishing students-as-citizens and universities as social institutions. Yet the value of the student's qualification is still understood and transacted in a social context. This chapter has argued that for public universities at least they have traditionally played a number of roles within the community and thus it has been more appropriate to conceive of the relationship between student and university within those broader contexts. This means that rather than conceptualizing the relationship as bilateral, involving only student and university, it is more accurate to conceptualize it as a trilateral relationship between student, university and community. One implication of this has been to recognize that not only do the expectations of each party change over time, but also that they can be at odds with each other. This leaves institutions with a major task in mediating these various expectations. A critical question for university managers as they face this shifting array of expectations from community and students is the extent to which they accept these shifts and adapt or the extent to which they challenge them. One choice that does not exist is to ignore them. In an era in which specialization is seen as the basis of performance, what is the value of generalist public teaching and research institutions who seek to meet the diverse needs and expectations of their students and other community stakeholders?

Acknowledgement

This chapter was prepared with the assistance of Catherine Burnheim.

Notes

1. Geoff Sharrock's unpublished essay "Why students are not (just) customers" provides this useful differentiation between customer transactions and a customer relationship.

2. One such example: at RMIT in the mid-1980s a compulsory sequence of subjects "Context Curriculum" was added to all undergraduate programs in an attempt to provide a contextual setting for the largely technically-oriented and vocationally-specific programs. By 2001 the initiative was virtually defunct, undermined by constant student complaint about disciplinary irrelevance and staff desires to exploit budget models that favoured in-faculty teaching. Yet this was an early attempt to avoid the criticism now prevalent from large employers that we produce technical robots.

References

ALFORD, J. (2002),
"Defining the Client in the Public Sector: A Social Exchange Perspective", *Public Administration Review*, Blackwell Publishers Inc., Boston and Oxford, Vol. 62, No. 3, pp. 337-346, May-June.

BARNETT, R. (2000),
"Reconfiguring the University", in P. Scott (ed.), *Higher Education Reformed*, Falmer Press, United Kingdom, pp. 114-129.

BIRRELL, B., CALDERON, A., DOBSON, I.R., and SMITH, T.F. (2000),
"Equity in Access to Higher Education Revisited", *People and Place*, 8(1), pp. 50-61.

BOWDEN, J. and MARTON, F. (1998),
The University of Learning, Kogan Page, London.

BURTON-JONES, A. (1999),
Knowledge Capitalism, Oxford University Press, New York.

BYRON, J. (2001),
"What Students Should Be Entitled to Expect from Universities", this volume, pp. 45-51.

COALDRAKE, P. (2000),
"Trends, Challenges and Opportunities", Paper to AVCC Senior Administrative Staff Conference, Tasmania, 25-27 October.

COALDRAKE, P. and STEDMAN, L. (2001),
"Responding to Changing Student Expectations", Background paper to OECD/IMHE seminar, QUT, Brisbane.

CORREA, H. (2001),
"A Game Theoretic Analysis of Faculty Competition and Academic Standards", *Higher Education Policy*, 14(2), pp. 175-182.

DUDERSTADT, J. (2001),
"A Tale of Two Futures" *http://milproj.ummu.umich.edu/publications/Future_of_University_3/sld001.htm*

DRUCKER, P. (1999),
"The New Pluralism", *Leader to Leader*, No. 19, Fall.

FARRINGTON, D. (2001),
"A Survey of Student-Institution Relationships in Europe", this volume, pp. 115-130.

GIBBONS, M. (1998),
Higher Education Relevance in the 21st Century, UNESCO World Conference on Higher Education, Paris, October 5-9.

HENDERSON, D. (2001),
"Undergraduate Student Perspectives of what students should be entitled to expect from universities", Paper to OECD/IMHE Conference on *Management Responses to Changing Student Expectations*, Brisbane, September.

JAMES, R. (2002),
"Students' Changing Expectations of Higher Education and the Consequences of Mismatches with the Reality", this volume, pp. 71-83.

MCINNIS, C. (2001),
"Signs of Disengagement? The Changing Undergraduate Experience in Australian Universities", *Inaugural Professorial Lecture*, Center for the Study of Higher Education, Faculty of Education, University of Melbourne.

MÜNSTEROVA, E., BASTOVA, J. and VLK, A. (2002),
"Case Study of the Students' View on the Educational Process and on University Management", this volume, pp. 53-69.

NEWMAN, F. (2000),
"A Faustian Bargain: How Does the University Save its Soul in the Entrepreneurial Age?", Paper to OECD/IMHE General Conference *Beyond the Entrepreneurial University*, Paris, September.

PASCARELLA, E. and TERENZINI, P. (1991),
"Studying College Students in the 21st Century: Meeting New Challenges", *The Review of Higher Education*, 21(2), pp. 151-65, Winter.

PUTNAM, R. (1993),
"The Prosperous Community", *The American Prospect*, 4(13), March 21.

SOMMERLAD, E. and STERN, E. (1998),
Workplace Learning, Learning Culture and Performance Improvement, Tavistock Institute, London.

WALSHOK, M. (1995),
Knowledge Without Boundaries – What America's Research Universities can do for the Economy, Workplace and the Community, Jossey-Bass, San Francisco.

Government Policy and Student Expectations: The Canadian Experience

Michael Conlon

This paper outlines the rapid change that Canada's system of post-secondary education has undergone in the past ten years. Though seen from a Canadian context, much of the comparative international research and dialogue of the Canadian Federation of Students leads me to believe that many of the changes outlined will have a familiar ring in Western Europe, New Zealand, Australia and the United States.

Throughout this chapter, an analysis of major policy shifts in post-secondary education policy is grafted onto an ongoing narrative of how these shifts have changed the relationship between students and universities. The analysis focuses on two areas: funding and privatisation. These areas represent two of the core policy dilemmas confronting Canadian universities and students. Though much of the account will focus on government policy, I will be making the case that this policy has had a decisive role in changing students' expectations and altering the relationship between students and universities.

A brief explanatory note is in order about Canada's system of post-secondary education. Unlike almost every other OECD country, Canada has no national Minister or Ministry of post-secondary education. Responsibility is hived off between several ministries with a separate Ministry roughly responsible for research, student financial assistance and core funding. The Canadian example is further complicated by the fact that though post-secondary education is largely funded by the Federal Government, jurisdiction over policy and specific funding allocation is in the hands of the ten provincial governments. Despite certain constitutional guarantees of mobility and universality there is substantial diversity among provinces over funding and policy goals. Nevertheless, despite inevitable local nuances, the Canadian example can provide some useful generalisations about student expectations.

Funding

Like most governments in the early 1990s, the Canadian government began cutting public services in the name of reducing the national deficit. Between 1993 and 1997 over CAD 7 billion was cut from post-secondary education and training. That cut translated into a reduction of 25% to the operating budget of Canadian universities and colleges. Students' share of the cost of education jumped from 16% in 1990 to 36% in 1998 and tuition fees increased by 126% in undergraduate arts and sciences programs. In many jurisdictions, tuition fees for professional programs such as law and medicine jumped from approximately CAD 3 000 to over CAD 12 000 in the space of three years.

The withdrawal of public funding also had the effect of dramatically increasing universities' reliance on private sources of funding. In 1990, 80% of core funding came from public sources. By 1998 it had declined to 64%. The portion that tuition fees comprise of university budgets increased from 18% to 30% between 1990 and 1998. During the same period, the proportion of corporate donations and gifts that comprise operating budgets jumped by 133%. The section on privatisation will address the operational and policy implications of increased corporate presence in the governance, research, and funding of higher education in Canada. For now, however, I simply want to outline the institutional responses to the substantial withdrawal of public funding (see CAUT, 2001).

The increase in tuition fees has resulted in several changes in institutional relations. First, the massive hike in fees has politicised students and united the student movement. Student unions have become much more politically active in the past ten years and this has resulted in greater representation and input into the governance of institutions. Though this push for representation has been resisted in some quarters, the sharp increase in fees has made it difficult for university administrators to resist calls for greater representation and accountability from students. Indeed the message from many students has been we will not pay upwards of 75% of the cost of our education (as do many students in professional programs like dentistry, computer science, and medicine) without a substantial say in the operation of programs.

This call for accountability has taken several forms. First, in the form of calls for increased representation on the highest decision making bodies of institutions. Second, in the form of faculty evaluations as well as students demanding a larger say in the evaluation of faculty performance and course material. In some cases, student unions have also initiated a call to have teaching performance be a greater part of tenure evaluation. A third and final implication of higher fees is an encroaching notion of students as consumers. This mentality has led to an upswing in consumer-like demands of institutions. In rare cases students have actually taken to suing institutions for failed expectations and allegedly shoddy performance on the part of an instructor or institution. For the most part, however, students have resisted the label of consumers and, ironically, one is more likely to hear such characterisations in the discourse of administrators.

The stance of the student movement in Canada has remained that education is a fundamental right in a democratic society that should be open to all with the ability and initiative to pursue it. If post-secondary education is to be seen as genuine marker of equality of opportunity it must remain universally accessible and, therefore, by definition affordable. The survival of a universal system of education depends on instilling a sense that it contributes to the public good and is, therefore, worthy of substantial public funds. The transfer of a large portion of funding to the individual via massive tuition fee hikes and the partial privatisation of the funding of higher education has contributed to this new discourse of consumerism in higher education. Again, however, it is critical to stress that this discourse has very little resonance among students, faculty, or the public at large.[1] Canadians still largely look to post-secondary education as a public good rather than a consumer service and, at a policy level, fights over tuition fees hikes and funding more often than not are a clash between competing visions of higher education's social meaning.

One policy development in which this differing vision has taken shape is in the creation of Register Education Savings Plans (RESP). RESPs allow an individual to shelter income from taxes while also receiving a 20% matching grant on all funds up to a maximum of CAD 2 000. The money set aside remains in trust in the child's name until he or she turns 18, at which time the funds must be used for post-secondary education costs. The marketing of the program is always accompanied by ominous, fatalistic predictions of ever increasing costs for higher education and the warning that failing to save now will exclude a child from pursuing a university education. The program has had several effects. First, it has implicitly undermined the notion of education of a collectively funded social good by moving the financial and political capital of the government to a scheme that rewards individual saving and funding of education. Further, the program has the political benefit of convincing people, however sub-consciously, that further fee hikes and funding cuts are not only inevitable but painless. Second, and more disturbing, it is a substantial transfer of funds to those who already have the means to save. Consider recent government data on the program. Of those from families of income less than CAD 30 000 per year, 80% said they wanted to save for a child's education, and of those only 19% reported that they actually were able to save. By contrast, among those with family income of over CAD 80 000, 95% reported a desire to save and of those 63% actually were saving (Statistics Canada, 2001).

The implications for participation and equity of access to higher education are disturbing. In the words of John Ralston Saul:

"Let's be clear about the effect of unsustainable cost and the resulting debts on individual students. Wherever tuition goes down, enrolment goes up. And where does the increase in students come from? From those with less money. In other words, the lower the fees, the more egalitarian the society. The lower the fees, the more we are able to release the genius of the citizenry as a whole. And that genius, that collective unconscious is the key to a successful democracy.[2]"

In December 2001, Statistics Canada released a national study which reported that individuals from the highest quartile income bracket (CAD 80 000 per year or more) were more than twice as likely to attend university as those in the lowest. Of those from families in the lowest quartile of income, 19% attended university; of those in the highest quartile, 39% attended university (Statistics Canada, 2002). Further, OECD data show that Canada along with France and Germany are the only OECD countries to see a decline in university participation rates over the past five years (OECD, 2001, Table C3.4).

Downloading the cost of post-secondary education to the individual has also put a marked strain on student financial assistance. Currently student loans are issued primarily through the publicly funded Canada Student Loan Program (CSLP). In 2000, 43% of Canadian students relied on loans to finance their education.

Student debt in Canada has risen from an average of CAD 8 000 in 1990 to CAD 25 000 in 1998.[3] During this time tuition fees rose by a national average of 126%. During that same period, student loan disbursements have increased from CAD 642 million in 1990 to over CAD 1.2 billion in 2001 (OCA, 2001). Currently 64% of monies issued through the Canada Student Loan Program are directed toward tuition fees. The Federal Government estimates that by 2025 that figure will climb to 91% (OCA, 2001, p. 21).

Privatisation

This section presents an analysis of the effect that decreased public funding and increased corporate donation has had on public post-secondary education in Canada.

For the Canadian student movement, the level of control exercised by corporations on the highest decision making body of Canadian institutions now represents a threat to their public mandate. In what follows, I want to trace what students see as the betrayal of the public trust by the increased corporate control of university governance. An account of the intense and disparate pressures bearing down on the public mandate of universities is vital to building an alternative and preserving the best elements of public colleges and universities. In this context, corporate governance refers to both the style of management and the dominance of the corporate community on board of governors. In particular, I want to explore the vital role that corporate governance has had in transforming the philosophy and practice of Canadian universities (CAUT, 1999).

In their ideal form, universities embody the social ambition of class mobility and equality of opportunity. In fact the ideal of class mobility and the goal of universal access marked the discourse surrounding the expansion of the Canadian University system in the 1960s. To the degree that these goals were achieved, the system of post-secondary education was based on the principle of collectively funded and publicly administered institutions. Public funding of post-secondary education was seen as indispensable if genuinely autonomous thought and research was to flourish in Canada. As public policy, it was also critical to have universities publicly administered because, in theory, one of their central missions was to promote universal access to post-secondary education regardless of income.

The current tension between public and private/corporate interests manifests itself in the schizophrenic climate in our institutions. On paper, universities remain guardians of the public interest but in reality universities are more and more accountable to their corporate donors. To my mind, this cultural clash is but a microcosm of the larger, global political program to eviscerate the principles and practice of publicly accountable institutions (Beaton, 1998). In short, the for-profit sector has set its sights on public institutions because the principle of public or collective good is generally anathema to profit. Civil society in any form except in its policing and incarceration functions has become the enemy and I do not think that we can separate this phenomenon from what is happening in our colleges and universities. In order to measure the political stakes of this conflict a more concrete analysis of the context and implications of the corporate governance of public post-secondary education institutions is in order.

The increased control exercised by corporations on governing boards is, ostensibly, the product of a happy historical and political co-incidence. The erosion of federal and provincial funding for post-secondary education provided an unprecedented opportunity for corporations to shape the direction of universities and to capitalise on the lucrative markets opened by the governing free market principle of less government that advocates the extinction of public institutions. At a practical level, the withdrawal of government funding has forced universities to rely on corporate "gifts" to fund basic operations. In return for such tax-deductible gifts, however, corporate Canada has been able to leverage a controlling interest in the governance of universities. This transition to corporately controlled boards of governors has not only changed the culture of institutions that are still largely publicly funded, it has also made Canadian universities vulnerable to dubious partnerships between industry and university researchers.

In addition to the obvious financial incentives, the slow, steady entrenchment of corporate values and practices was precipitated by several interrelated factors. The establishment in 1983 of the Corporate-Higher Education Forum (CHEF) and the findings of the Macdonald Commission, also in 1983, heralded the need for

41

the corporate sector to have more ready and cost effective access to the leading edge knowledge produced by universities. The CHEF was established to strengthen ties between the corporate community and the university community. The composition of the CHEF boasted CEOs from companies such as Shell, Xerox, Royal Bank, and Nortel. In addition, the CHEF also has the active participation of most university presidents. The creation of the CHEF was an early realisation that the shift from a resource-based economy to a knowledge-based economy made universities a prime target for profit. Of course, corporations have always aspired to footholds on university campuses but the historical shift in economic activity provided the means and opportunity for a full frontal assault on the public mandate of Canadian universities. The shift towards a knowledge-based economy and the federal withdrawal of funding for post-secondary education made universities an irresistible financial and political target for corporate Canada (Newson and Buchbinder, 1988, p. 59).

The business strategy driving this political agenda is motivated by growth opportunities for the private sector in two particular areas. First, the profit potential contained in the generation of intellectual property. As John Roth, President of Nortel, put it: "the University is the source of our continuous renewal. From primary to post-graduate levels, science and technology ... are the key to Nortel's success" (Schmidt, 1998). Second, the profit potential in the private, for-profit delivery and administration of post-secondary education itself. At the recent World Trade Organisation talks held in Seattle, Washington, Canada refused to rule out the possibility of negotiating greater trade liberalisation in the private delivery of post-secondary education. However, in a legal opinion obtained by the Canadian Federation of Students and the Canadian Association of University Teachers, the GATS framework that Canada has already signed onto will likely impair their ability to protect public post-secondary education from private "competition".[4] In essence, the argument is that public post-secondary education precludes the possibility of post-secondary education being delivered like any other for-profit service. If that logic prevails it will be hard to argue that publicly funded post-secondary education does not hold unfair or "illegal" advantage over private for-profit education providers. Indeed, both New Zealand and the United States have staked out aggressive strategies for the liberalisation of trade in post-secondary education and training in the latest rounds of GATS negotiations.

To conclude, then, changing student expectations are the product of a paradigm shift in the way in which governments and university administrators have come to view post-secondary education. As noted earlier, one of the principles behind publicly funded universities is the social goal of universality. By and large students in Canada are struggling to maintain this sense of universality in the face of the encroaching view of education as a largely individual and hence individualistic enterprise. Canadian students, therefore, frame their institutional

42

expectations on the ideal of the university as a space of collective learning and remembering. These expectations, then, are defined and measured by the equality of opportunity our universities provide for all.

Notes

1. In a poll conducted for the Canadian Federation of Students by Ipsos Reid in November 2001, over 82% of respondents thought tuition fees were already too high. This supports findings from a variety of other polls that the public has very little appetite for high tuition fees. The Ipsos Reid poll can be viewed at *www.cfs-fcee.ca*

2. These remarks come from a commencement address delivered at Simon Fraser University, 5 October 2000. A copy of the full text of the remarks was delivered to the Canadian Federation of Students.

3. See the Federal Government's Budget Plan 1998 (*www.canoe.ca*/FedBudgetMirror/*pamphe/ studpae.html*). There are few recent student debt totals available, but since 1998 fees have continued to rise with no additional non-repayable student financial assistance.

4. A copy of this legal opinion, obtained from trade law firm Gottlieb and Pearson is available at *www.cfs-fcee.ca*. A précis of the opinion is also available at the same address.

References

BEATON, J.B. (1998),
   The Commercialisation of Universities in Canada: Corporate University Relations, York University, Toronto.

CANADIAN ASSOCIATION OF UNIVERSITY TEACHERS (CAUT) (1999),
   Universities and Colleges in the Public Interest – Research Report 1 and 2.

CANADIAN ASSOCIATION OF UNIVERSITY TEACHERS (CAUT) (2001),
   "University and College Affordability: How and why have fees increased", CAUT *Education Review*, 3(2), pp. 1-11.

NEWSON, J. and BUCHBINDER, H. (1988),
   The University Means Business, Garamond Press, Toronto.

OFFICE OF THE CHIEF ACTUARY (OCA) (2001),
   Actuarial Report: Canada Student Loan Program as at July 31, 2001.

ORGANISATION FOR ECONOMIC CO-OPERATION AND DEVELOPMENT (OECD) (2001),
   Education at a Glance: OECD Indicators, OECD, Paris.

SCHMIDT, S. (1998),
   "Wired world has design on ivory tower", *Varsity News*, March 17.

STATISTICS CANADA (2001),
   Survey of Approaches to Education Planning, April 10.

STATISTICS CANADA (2002),
   Erratum to *Participation in post-secondary education and family income*, January 9.

What Should Students Be Entitled to Expect From Universities?

A Postgraduate Perspective

John Byron

The benefit of soliciting the student perspective on any aspect of higher education policy seems obvious, but unfortunately this enlightened attitude is not ubiquitous. Indeed, consultation with students is among the key expectations that we hold of our institutions. But before launching into my list of things students feel entitled to expect from their institutions – my log of claims, as it were – I would like to address a couple of points of clarification.

The first thing is that the relationships between students and their institutions are and probably always have been very complex. They are also manifold, and hugely diverse, so that statements made about the relationships must be understood to refer to a range of extant relationships, several of which any given student simultaneously holds. Nonetheless, with this caveat in place it is possible to tease out a few main ways that students relate to their institutions.

Fundamentally there is a pedagogical relationship, which includes the initiation into a discipline of learning, the passing on of skills, the sharing of ways of seeing and ways of thinking, and the like. Equally important is the civic relationship that governs the student's induction into participation in the life of public institution. Particularly with younger students there is a considerable pastoral relationship. In the case of postgraduate students there is very often an industrial relationship. Higher degree research students enjoy a marked collegial relationship, and are potential colleagues as well as students.

Students interact with their institutions collectively as well as individually. They encounter their institutions politically, as well as through cultural and sporting contexts. There is a commercial relationship between students and their institutions particularly in the case of fee paying students but also in the case of those paying HECS or even those on scholarships. Students are active subjects in their educational experiences, as well as objects in relationship between institutions and government or commercial entities.

I don't plan here to try to tease out all of the implications for the topic of this project of this manifold relationship between students and their institutions. However, in a very real sense, it is this complexity itself that is *the* defining characteristic of the student experience. Larger than the sum of its parts, the student experience is probably so memorable and formative as well as so ineffable simply because its essence *is* this very complexity. While it may upset those who tried to modify reality to fit the dry bones of a dominant economic, social or political theory, this "messiness" is really the flesh of the lived experience of students. I point this out because of the potential danger that thinking along the lines that are framing this discussion may lead us to overdetermine the implications of the legal and commercial relationship between students in institutions.

Lately it has become fashionable to quote Edmund Burke, even among those who sit on the treasury benches and are doing their level best to extinguish humanities disciplines such as political philosophy. Not wishing to surrender Burke to the conservatives – on occasion he had some useful things to say to others among us – I would refer to an oft-quoted line from his address to the electors of Bristol in 1774. Burke declared, "Your representative owes you, not his industry only, but his judgement; and he betrays instead of serving you if he sacrifices it to your opinion". Presumably this dictum applies to women as readily as to men. Additionally, I would argue that this is true of leadership in general, and not just democratic representation.

Being a teacher is a form of leadership. A good teacher is a very special kind of leader, who does not wield power so much as authority; who leads by example, not by prescription; who places greater emphasis on method that content; who fosters leadership in others rather than defending herself from it. A good teacher is consultative and responsive, but always exercises her judgement, rather than bowing to raw opinion.

To flesh out where we are going here, I would like to introduce a few propositions that can help underwrite the argument put by this chapter:

- The market does not necessarily know what is good for it.
- Even when it does, the market is not necessarily equipped to procure what is good for it.
- The customer is not always right.
- Neither is the vendor.
- Consumer-driven changes are not necessarily beneficial to consumers.
- Competition policy can ultimately expose consumers to fewer choices and higher prices than a well-managed centrally regulated structure.
- Education is transformative – of societies, as well as of students.
- Expectations, in order to be meaningful, must be informed.

- There are some processes that we undergo, the outcomes of which it is not possible to measure or even understand, before the fact.

- A process of learning involves or even demands entrusting oneself to the greater knowledge and methodological proficiency of our teachers.

Taking these propositions together, I am trying to give a sense that students expect to be taken on a journey that to a considerable degree they cannot imagine at the outset. They expect to have input during the journey, because this is the only way they can learn to be anything other than passengers. But they do not expect to call the shots, to be given only what it is that they have the experience to ask for, or to be regarded simply as revenue sources.

It has been said that some students want a university experience that is quick, easy and cheap. Perhaps some individual students do, but I would like to emphatically declare that students at large want an education, not a drive-through degree. When university is presented as being primarily about credentialing, then the expectation of cheap and nasty automatic pass degree factories is reasonable – destructive and self-defeating, but logically consistent, because the experience is already devoid or depleted of value. But when universities, employers and the community at large continue to emphasise the education itself, then rigour and substance are valued, and the *testamur* is merely the sign or trace of the educational achievement. In these conditions, the wish for a cheap and nasty experience is unreasonable, and surely this is the outcome we are looking to achieve.

Some individual students may prefer to score an effortless pass on a lightweight course to get the piece of paper they think they paid for. Collectively though, students recognise that what we are paying for – in fees, in hard work, in income forgone – is both the educational experience itself, and the universities' endorsement of a genuine achievement. Clearly soft marking in dodgy courses, or the tolerance of plagiarism, satisfy neither of these defining characteristics of education. It is not in the interests of students past present or future for universities to erode the standards in courses, to compromise on quality, or to otherwise pander to a perceived – and perhaps imagined – preference on the part of prospective students for ease, entertainment, and automatic certification. It is therefore not a paradox that students expect universities to deny authority to market whim, even when they themselves are perceived to be the market. Of course such a policy takes guts, especially in an increasingly commercialised, competitive context.

So students expect leadership from their universities. They expect it in the sense just outlined, but in other ways too. They expect their universities to refuse to accept as reasonable levels of funding that make it impossible for them to discharge their obligations as public institutions. Students expect university leaders to speak out when they judge conditions to be dire. And students are prepared to support their university leaders when they make unpopular statements about the conditions under which they are trying to function.

Students expect each institution to understand that its work is done on behalf of, and for the benefit of, the public at large – in the national interest if you like – which includes in different ways: government, industry, the environment, the global community, and parents, as well as students themselves.

As mentioned at the outset, students expect to be consulted on matters affecting them. They expect that their representative organisations should be treated with respect and regarded as a valuable resource. They expect to have input on the committees, boards and councils that manage universities.

Students expect that their own leaders and representatives will be able to develop a relationship with university leaders that is characterised by partnership, collaboration, discussion, respect, and proper influence. They expect that their institutional roles will be governed by the principles of collegiality and community. One university leader told me recently that, while student representatives were annoying, he regarded this as our job. "When you come in here, eight times out of ten you talk rubbish", he said. "Only one time out of ten do I agree with you. But the other one time I disagree with you, and it later turns out you were right."

Students expect their institutions to recognise the value of diversity. Universities should embrace and foster diversity, which is not a problematic new characteristic demanding uncomfortable changes: rather cultural diversity is Australia's edge in global education market. Australia is brilliantly positioned to exploit its very unusual cultural diversity, and to mistake this strength for a liability would be a terrible blindness for us to suffer. Introducing and promoting measures to assist people currently underrepresented in higher education is one of the hallmarks of a management scheme designed to encourage genuine innovation.

Students expect their institutions to implement and promote equity measures, including affirmative action measures, to enable academic participation profiles to match those in society. They expect universities to value the critical and fundamentally beneficial consequences of a student body that mirrors the diversity of our society. When you write policy as though everyone is white, middle-class, financially stable, English-speaking, urban, mobile, straight, and right-handed, then sooner or later that is what your student body starts looking like, as those who deviate from the norm are squeezed out.

Students expect that their institutions will apply rigorous entry standards based on genuinely informed indicators of academic talents and potential. Like their first-year tutors, students well know from intimate experience that the least useful indicator of scholastic ability is one's access to cold, hard cash. They expect that institutions will maintain such rigorous standards – and not merely the appearance of high standards – throughout their degrees, and into the future, in order to maintain the value of their hard-won qualifications.

Students expect their institutions to live up to their promises. They expect to be treated with respect when being recruited. They expect to be able to believe what they are told. They expect universities to commit to a relationship, not to just turn on the charm until they get what they want.

Students expect to be supported, encouraged, and guided. Higher degree research students for instance, expect to participate in a practical and enabling induction program. They expect to be adequately resourced, not least so they can deliver on their side of the research and writing bargain. They also expect to be welcomed as colleagues in their departments, to start to participate in the life of their institutions, and to be inducted into the development of their disciplines.

Coursework postgraduates expect to be taught at a level of engagement that is equivalent to honours standard at certificates and diploma level, and well above it at masters level. This may sound obvious, but they expect to be lectured, tutored, and assessed at this appropriate level, and not appended as cost-neutral revenue raisers to undergraduate classes. They do not expect to be regarded primarily as a source of a valuable cross-subsidy for the other activities of the university in the context of the significant decline in federal government operating grant.

Students expect academic boards to persist with successful methodologies and pedagogical practices even though they may be unpopular (the dreaded but very successful tutorial paper is a good example). Such judgements, of course, must be based on genuine evidence, and not on mere unwillingness to change.

Students expect new methodologies and practices to be adopted, even when they are unpopular. Such judgements, of course, must also be based on genuine evidence, and not on mere fashionable change.

Students expect their institutions to imagine them not as a category to be "dealt with" by the university, but as a group that is fundamentally a part of the university. Institutions must not lose sight of the fact that education will never be like other client relationships, because the student experiences herself *qua* student also as a worker, a participant, an owner, a resident, a manager, and a life-long member of a family.

Students expect their universities to recognise that public institutions are established to discharge a commission bestowed upon them by the polity, and that their success, therefore, is measured by outcomes, not by income.

Students expect their institutions to understand that, when their marketers make claims about the product changing lives, they happen to be telling the truth. Soft drinks and running shoes will not change your life, but a good education certainly will.

Institutions should also understand that the brand is not the product; rather, the education itself is the product. As graduates and students, we are entitled to own a little of the brand, in the letters after our names and the parchments on our walls. This brand-sharing is not the life-changing thing itself, but just its trace, its sign.

Students expect each institution to understand that it does not own the brand. Staff and students – past, present and future – and the community at large own the brand, because it is they who give it value. Students expect their institutions to remember this when tempted to sell the brand, or to rent it out, or to mortgage it.

Students also expect institutions to defend the value of resource-intensive methods, even when they cannot afford to offer them due to the depletion of resources. Students expect universities to understand that their unmet expectations are not necessarily unreasonable – that they may be unmet because of someone else's misunderstanding of what it takes to operate a university system and to deliver an adequate education, and not the students' misunderstanding.

Students understand that resource cuts can impair quality to the point of crisis, and – despite countervailing opinion – they know that just about everybody who actually works in the system recognises that this is actually the case at present. They expect their institutional leaders to be champions of a properly resourced and intelligently managed education system.

Students do not expect to be reassured that cheaper substitute methods or processes are adequate when they are not. They expect instead to be partners in the attempt to demand something better for our students, our academics, our community, and our future.

Students expect that their institutions will defend the value of independent, autonomous, and active student organisations. The expect that institutions will see that their representative organisations give universities for free what mercantile concerns have to pay large sums of money for – feedback, advice, requests, input, and a clear window on the reality (palatable or not) of the moods and experiences of their student bodies.

Students expect institutions to know that – to slightly misquote Ridley Scott's 1982 film *Blade Runner* – "We're not in the business of education: we *are* the business of education."

I hope that this round-up of the postgraduate perspective on the question of what students can expect from their institutions has established that, in our sector, we are all singing from the same songbook. Despite the activities of the few, the engagement in a high quality education is still the paramount demand that students and the community place upon universities. Despite the activities of a different few, we are not impressed with the notion that this is fundamentally or even significantly a commercial relationship. Students enter into university with a sense of wonder and enthusiasm to be taken beyond themselves; we urge administrators, government and policy-makers to refrain from creating the conditions in which wonder ceases, and the self cannot be transcended, due to a demeaning and diminishing reliance upon direct funding from some sort of bastardised pupil-benefactor.

Universities must lead, and decline to do otherwise. Students deserve, require, and expect nothing less.

A Case Study of the Students' View on the Educational Process and on University Management

Eva Münsterova, Jarmila Bastova and Ales Vlk

Introduction

The focus of this chapter is:

- To glance at the higher education system in the Czech Republic.
- To explain the institutional position of students in Czech higher education institutions.
- To show the ways by which students can assert their rights and demands.
- To give examples of how students' affairs are dealt with by two nation-wide institutions [one elective – Council of Higher Education Institutions (CHEI), one state-based – Centre for Higher Education Studies (CHES)].

An historical note

Until the Second World War, and shortly after, the Czech Republic was highly regarded as a democratic and well-developed country in terms of education, culture, science and industry. Then, for about forty years, it was a part of the Eastern Bloc. This period severely influenced the whole of society and people's lives. Over the last decade, great effort has been made to overcome this adverse heritage and to restore earlier positive aspects. While the older and present generations have started this process, only the new generation – if well educated – will possess enough time and power to bring it to fruition. We are also aware of the fact that students have many a time played a significant role in circumstances of major historical importance. That is why they are considered important, and given significant freedom and rights.

Rapid and fundamental changes have taken place in tertiary education in the Czech Republic since the 1990s, and continue today. The intensity and profundity of these changes have brought many completely new and specific problems that need to be solved by legislative and other means. In this process it must be kept in mind that in the tertiary sector it is adult people who are being educated, who have full legal responsibility and independence in decision making. Strong motivation and a responsible approach towards education are taken for granted, and it is assumed that students should have an appropriate influence on the operations of educational institutions.

Legislation on higher education in the Czech Republic

Legislation referring to higher education in the Czech Republic includes:

National Acts:

- Act No. 111/1998 Coll. on Higher Education Institutions and on Modification and Amendment of Other Acts (The *Higher Education Act*).

- Amendment of Act No. 111/1998 Coll. included in the Act No. 147/2001 Coll.

These Acts replaced the previous Act on higher education, No. 172/1990 Coll. that was amended in 1993. The actual Acts are extraordinarily modern and liberal. According to them, most of the previous State higher education institutions have been changed to public ones and have gained great autonomy. Students have been given unusual rights to share this autonomy and to derive benefit from it. One part of the Act is devoted directly to the students' issues. It states what requirements an adept must meet to become a student, introduces the rights and duties of the student, and instructs on how to decide about these and how to judge disciplinary misdemeanours. Among the students' rights there are some interesting ones. The student is entitled to study free of charge within the framework of one or several study programmes, to choose a teacher for a subject of study lectured by several teachers, to enrol free of charge in the next part of the study programme upon fulfilling given requirements, to elect members and to be elected as a member of the academic senate, and to be granted a scholarship from the financial funds of the higher education institution upon fulfilling given conditions.

National documents agreed by the Government:

- Conception of Education and Development of Education System in the Czech Republic (1999).

- National Policy in Research and Development (1999).

- Conception of the State Information Policy in Education (2000).

- National Programme of Education Development in the Czech Republic (the so-called White Book) (2000).

International agreements and declarations:

- Convention on the Recognition of Qualifications concerning Higher Education in the European Region (Lisbon Convention, 1997).

- Sorbonne Declaration (1998).

- Bologna Declaration (1999).

- Prague Communiqué (2001).

The main institutions representing the higher education system in the Czech Republic

Some of the main institutions are introduced in Figure 1. The internal structure of a public higher education institution is set out in Figure 2.

The system of higher education is headed by the **Ministry of Education, Youth and Sports (MEYS)** with its **Division of Science and Higher Education (DSHE)**. The scope of authority of the Ministry is given by the Act.

Under the authority of the DSHE falls the **Centre for Higher Education Studies (CHES)**, a State research organisation consisting of a Research Department, the National Centre for Distance Learning, the Centre for Equivalence of Documents about Education, and the national office of European Union (EU) education programmes. The CHES deals systematically with current as well as prospective problems of the development of tertiary education. The research of CHES marginally intersects and complements the work of other institutes founded by the MEYS (*i.e.* the Education Research Institute in Prague, the National Institute of Technical and Vocational Education, and the Institute for Information in Education), although the research activities of these latter institutes are not directly related to higher education issues. The same applies to the Institute of Research and Development in Education that belongs to the Faculty of Education of the Charles University in Prague.

The **Accreditation Commission (AC)** is an independent formal advisory body of the Minister. The AC evaluates activities pursued by higher education institutions and the quality of accredited activities. It assesses other issues pertaining to the system of higher education presented to it by the Minister. It makes rulings on requests for accreditation of study, and requests for authorisation to perform habilitation procedures or procedures for the appointment of professors, and over any change concerning the number and kind of faculties of a public or state higher education institution. It also issues statements concerning the granting of State permission for a legal entity desiring to operate as a private higher education institution, and for determining the type of a higher education institution.

Figure 1.   **Overview of the main institutions connected with higher education**

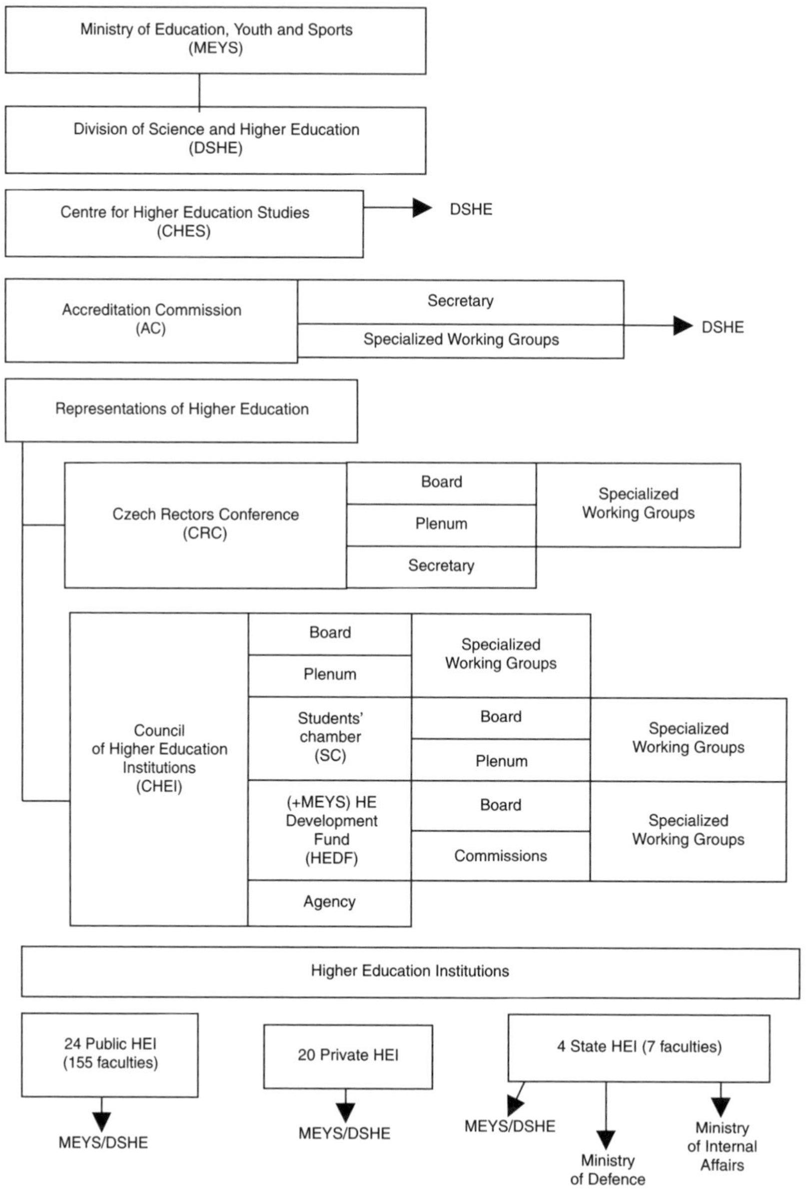

Source: Authors.

© OECD 2002

Figure 2. **The internal structure of a Czech public higher education institution**

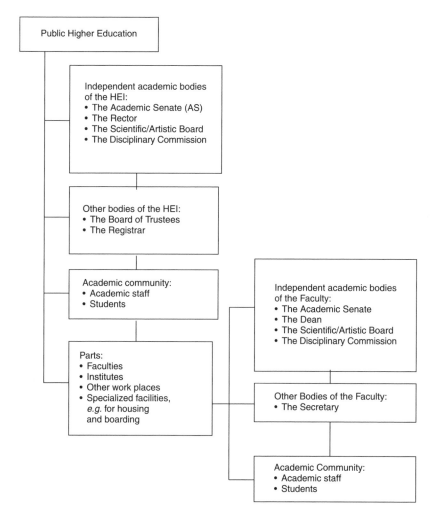

Source: Authors.

Representative bodies of higher education institutions: the Czech Rectors Conference (CRC) is a body composed of the representatives of higher education institutions, and the Council of Higher Education Institutions (CHEI) comprises members of academic communities of institutions delegated by their representative academic bodies, *i.e.* Academic Senates. These representations are the two principal bodies acting in the interest of the higher education institutions. Their main concern is the strategic development of the higher education system, including management, economy, education, and research, as well as legal and institutional conditions of all aspects of university life. They co-operate in a close and creative way, in spite of some differences of opinion expressed on certain occasions. They offer informal advice to the Minister, with whom they discuss proposals and measures that have a significant impact on higher education institutions.

The essential part of the tertiary education sector is comprised of **higher education institutions.** They are the highest components of the education system and the leading centres of knowledge. The principal activity of higher education institutions is teaching, inseparably connected with research and development, and other creative and art activities. Public and State institutions differ from the private universities in the way of financing (State appropriation without tuition fees for the former, and tuition fees from students and no money from the State for the latter). All study programmes, irrespective of the kind of higher education institution, are subjected to accreditation by the Ministry.

In connection with the primary issue of this paper, it is desirable to explain the structure, rights and duties of the **Academic Senates (AS)**, which represent the autonomy of academic communities within each institution and each of their faculties. The Academic Senate of the institution consists of at least eleven members, with at least one third and at most one half being students. The members of the Academic Senate are elected from the academic community for a term that may not exceed three years. The meetings of the Academic Senate are open to the public. According to the Act, the Academic Senate of a public higher education institution performs the following tasks:

- Upon the recommendation of the Rector, it makes decisions on any change concerning the number and kind of individual parts of the institutions.
- It approves internal regulations of the institution and its parts.
- It approves the budget of the institution presented by the Rector and supervises the deployment of the financial resources of the institution.
- It approves the annual report on activities and annual report on economic management of the institution presented by the Rector.
- It approves evaluation of the institution presented by the Rector.
- It approves the Rector's proposals for nominating and dismissing members of the Scientific Board and the Disciplinary Commission of the institution.
- It approves conditions for admission to studies in those study programmes not provided by individual faculties.
- It resolves upon proposals for nominating or dismissing the Rector.
- It approves long-term goals in the area of the main activities of the institution and their annual updates.

Besides these tasks, the Academic Senate makes statements upon certain subjects. The Academic Senate of the Faculty exercises similar duties with respect to the faculty.

The role of students in the higher education system of the Czech Republic

As the above statements have shown, the higher education system in the Czech Republic involves a democratic conglomeration of duties, rights and services.

The institutional position of students as equal partners in academic communities is guaranteed by the Act, in which the rights and duties of the students are clearly expressed. The students' institutional power to influence the everyday life of higher education institutions is relatively high. It is derived primarily from the great number of student representatives in the Academic Senates of the faculties and higher education institutions, from the existence of the students' chamber of CHEI and from the various rights and duties these bodies have, as outlined earlier. It is well known that many students in these representative bodies are devoted to their mission and work highly effectively. It is highly appreciated that they want to be a part of the common representative bodies, together with the academic staff.

Unfortunately, a noticeable gap exists between the students' representatives on one side, and the mass of the students on the other. Many students are not tightly connected with the common problems of the institution and do not care for solving them, unless they are personally affected. Often they even do not know their representatives, and do not appreciate the work done by them. This situation should be addressed and gradually altered, to teach students how to participate in the social life of the institution.

On the other hand, in spite of the modern Act and institutional policy, students often have to face personal situations and reactions which emphasise their subsidiary position in the academic community. A lot of work still remains to be done on both sides, among academic staff as well as among students to make this situation better.

How the CHEI concerns itself with student issues

The CHEI relies on the co-operation of its expert committees, which deal with various legislative, economic, educational and research issues. The students' representatives take part in every expert committee of the CHEI together with the academics.

Among others there exists an expert committee concerned with the creative activities of students. It endeavours to establish better co-operation between students and academic staff with respect to education, research and management.

Lectures and seminars have been organised by the expert committee on this issue. To give an example, the nation-wide conference "valuation of the Education Activities at Higher Education Institutions from the Students' Point of View" as held in 1998 in Brno. Participants included both academics and students. The aim of this conference was to explain the basic aspects of this issue, to make it more acceptable to the teachers and to show its limitations to students. Eminent specialists in pedagogy, philosophy, psychology, sociology and law presented lectures, including:

- Student evaluation of teaching activities.
- Foreign experiences on evaluating the educational process.
- "Teacher-student" interactions in the process of evaluation.
- Psychological aspects of the evaluation of the teacher done by students.
- Latent dysfunction of the standardised evaluation methods.
- Validity of the evaluation of teaching process.
- Feedback mechanisms joined to the evaluation of the teaching process.
- Students self-evaluation.
- Are the students interested in the evaluation of the teaching process?
- Communication between teachers and students: feedback and the strategy "I'm OK, you're OK".
- A few case-studies reflecting the evaluation and assessment of quality of the teaching process at several universities in the Czech Republic.

The other important role the expert committee is expected to play is to support and monitor the research and creative activities of students at the higher education institutions.

Of course, the Students Chamber of the CHEI deals with most of the students' issues.

The Students Chamber succeeded in gaining membership of foreign student organisations, namely.

- In 2000, the Central European Students Network, responsible for student mobility;
- In 2001, the National Unions of Students in Europe (ESIB), the task of which is to implement the ideas of the Bologna Declaration; and
- In 2001, the expert commission Committee for Prague 2001 (Prague Summit).

Owing to membership in these organisations, students took part in several European meetings and conferences on higher education. In this way they gain experience from abroad.

The expert committees of the Students Chamber also co-operated in the preparation of and research for some important documents, *e.g.*:

- Act No. 111/1998 Coll. and its Amendment No. 147/2001 Coll.
- The National Programme of Education Development in the Czech Republic (so-called White Book) (2000).
- The Statute of CHEI and Order of Proceeding of the Students Chamber.
- Guidelines for admitting foreign students to higher education institutions in the Czech Republic.
- Requirements for Ph.D. studies.

There also exist some difficult issues being dealt with by the Students Chamber. Students are now preparing their basic standpoint regarding the overall situation of higher education. The students wish higher education to be widely diversified and open to all adepts, and they favour the idea of mobility. On the other hand, students oppose paying tuition fees. Some of these ideas coincide with public opinion, some do not. Therefore much discussion is to be expected in the academic communities and in wider society with respect to these topics.

The activities of the Centre for Higher Education Studies (CHES)

Students do not belong to the staff of the CHES. However, they often appear there as participants in seminars or in teamwork upon certain issues. They also often come to acquire information and advice, or to be supervised while preparing their diploma work or dissertation.

The research department of this institution has for many years paid systematic attention to student issues. Staff have examined the influence of macro structural changes in society on the social status of higher education students. A sociological survey in 1991 dealt with the impact of social transformation on the everyday life of students, and of the changes in conditions of higher education studies. In 1994, a sociological survey of secondary schools was conducted, which paid attention to the issue of access to education, and to the analysis of study motivations and expectations of secondary school students, as far as their insertion in the labour market is concerned. The Centre has conducted two surveys in 1997, namely *Opinions of Students and Graduates of Law Faculties on their University Study*, and the *Insertion of Graduates of* VSB – *Technical University in Practice*. A major sociological survey conducted by CHES involved a long-term study of the social status of higher education students in the Czech Republic. It was carried out in three stages:

- 1992 – Social Status of Higher Education Students;
- 1996 – Social Portrait of Higher Education Students in the Czech Republic; and
- 1999 – Social Portrait of Higher Education Students in the Czech Republic.

A nation-wide sociological research project was prepared in 2001 and carried out in 2002.

The questions themselves as well as their results in the year 1999 are very interesting and worth discussing. Among them:

- **Characteristics** of the participating students: 3 036 students as a whole, 45% men, 55% women. 86.7% of students were single, 11% lived with a partner.

- **The percentage distribution** of participating students according to their faculty.

Table 1.   **Distribution of all students among types of higher education institution in the Czech Republic**

Faculties	Percentage	Faculties	Percentage
Medical	7.3	Humanitarian	13.3
Pedagogical	16.9	Technical	28.7
Law	5.3	Agricultural	5.9
Economics	17.4	Natural sciences	5.2

The questions asked

The faculty you are studying at is	Percentage
Where you really wanted to study	62.1
Compensatory but still acceptable to you	33.2
An emergency choice	4.7

In case of a new opportunity you will choose	Percentage
The same faculty you are studying at	67.6
Other faculty	28.7
Other way of education, different from higher education	2.6
No education after secondary school-leaving exam	1.1

Are you satisfied with general study conditions at your faculty?	Percentage
I am satisfied, I consider them to be good	9.3
I am satisfied, but with some objections	59.3
I am not very satisfied, I have serious objections	29.3
I am quite unsatisfied, I consider them to be bad	2.1

Source: CHES, 1999.

There is no space here to discuss these results. But at least they can be used as a background for the following case study at the Brno University of Technology.

Table 2. **Evaluation of general study conditions according to the type of faculties**

Percentage

Faculties	Definitely satisfied	Rather satisfied	Rather dissatisfied	Definitely dissatisfied
Medical	5.4	68.3	24.0	2.3
Pedagogical	9.2	64.5	23.8	2.5
Law	22.0	54.7	22.6	0.7
Economics	15.2	69.3	14.2	1.3
Humanities	14.9	57.7	24.5	3.0
Technical	21.4	61.5	16.3	0.8
Agricultural	12.2	66.1	21.1	0.6
Natural sciences	7.6	58.2	34.0	3.8

To what extent do the next statements indicate the situation at your faculty?	Yes	No
The majority of lectures is satisfactory and interesting	68.6	31.4
Quality of lessons is improved by foreign teachers	30.2	69.8
Students may discuss and defend their own opinions during lectures	61.3	38.7
Sufficient attention is paid to improving language competence	41.0	59.0
Students may choose subjects of study to design their individual curriculum	54.2	45.8
Possibility to study abroad	54.7	45.3
Textbooks are available in a sufficient amount	45.8	54.2
Necessary learning aids are very expensive	76.2	23.8
The classrooms are big enough	63.9	36.1

What do you think about teaching at your faculty?	Yes	No
It is well organised, without time losses	59.9	40.1
It gives broad basic knowledge	81.0	19.0
It affords good possibilities of specialisation	64.6	35.4
It affords good possibilities of using information technologies	44.6	55.4
Duplicate knowledge often occurs	49.6	50.4
The student may choose the exam-terms suitable for him	65.2	34.8
Preference is given to quality, not to quantity of knowledge	42.7	57.3
Sufficient space is given for self-learning	49.3	50.7
Students learn to know the up-date knowledge	64.0	36.0
Teaching is not only theoretical, it offers some practical skills	51.6	48.4

What is your experience with higher education teachers?	Predominantly yes	Predominantly no
They respect students as partners	78.4	21.6
Their pedagogic abilities are very good	66.2	33.8
They are experts in their branch	82.9	17.1
They now the praxis well	59.5	40.5
They are well-prepared for giving lectures and leading seminars	87.8	12.2
They are always prepared to give professional advice	80.5	19.5
They are aware of the abilities of the individual student	23.1	76.9
They see and understand personal problems of students	51.5	48.5
They keep tutorial hours	76.5	23.5
They do not prefer their other personal activities to teaching	67.3	32.7

Source: CHES, 1999.

63

Case study at the Brno University of Technology (BUT)

The Brno University of Technology

History: The Brno University of Technology is one of the oldest universities in the Czech Republic. Its origin dates back to 1849 when a German-Czech Technical School was established in Brno. In the years 1872 and 1873, the School was awarded the status of a university. A Czech Technical University was founded in Brno in 1899. Before the start of the World War I there were already four departments (civil, mechanical, electrical and chemical engineering). Between World War I and World War II, the Czech Technical University ranked among the best technical universities in Europe with many foreign students. During World War II the University was, as were all other Czech universities, closed. After the War, the Czech Technical University was re-opened. In 1951, the bulk of the University was transformed into the Military Technical Academy. The civilian Technical University was re-established in 1956. In 1992 the Faculty of Business and Management and the Faculty of Chemistry were established, and one year later the Faculty of Arts was constituted. In 1999, the name Brno University of Technology was introduced.

Teaching and learning: The BUT provides education in Bachelors and Masters degrees, and PhD study programmes which cover the whole spectrum of technical disciplines in mechanical engineering, civil engineering, electrical engineering and computer science, chemistry and chemical engineering, as well as disciplines in the field of economics and management, architecture, design and fine arts. The University devotes attention to developing interdisciplinary branches such as materials science and engineering, mechatronics, mathematical, physical and ecological engineering.

About 14 000 students are enrolled at seven faculties. Teaching at the University takes place in the atmosphere of research. BUT has implemented a credit system which is compatible with ECTS. This is one of the conditions for the University to join the ERASMUS programme.

The University Development Plan sets out a shift of emphasis from teaching to student learning. Students' academic work is increasingly characterised by project work and other forms of self-directed study, and is supported by the library system of the University. Seven faculty libraries co-ordinated by the BUT Central Library provide professional services.

Science and research: BUT is a research university. Main research activities are concentrated into eighteen long-term research programme across the academic areas mentioned above.

Co-operation with industry: Rapidly developing co-operation with industrial companies is based on a well-balanced partnership, in which both parties influence one another and direct development towards high technology areas. BUT is working purposefully on preparing conditions for commercial utilisation of the university's know-how, transfer of technologies and support of innovative activities.

BUT is a founding member of the Forum of Czech Industry and Universities and a member of the Innovative Enterprise Association. It co-operates with the Industry and Transport Association and with the Association of Building Industry Entrepreneurs, and is a member of the Chamber of Commerce, and is taking part in construction of the Brno Technology Park.

International co-operation: International study at the BUT is supported by EU-financed projects (TEMPUS, ERASMUS, CEEPUS) that allow reciprocal student and teacher mobility. They also contribute to evaluation and comparison of study programmes and conditions and rating criteria at BUT, and to co-operation with foreign universities.

There are also projects that offer studies awarding two diplomas (from BUT and a foreign university), Euro-engineer degree, or PhD studies with one local and one foreign tutor.

Lectures are given by visiting professors to allow the exchange of expertise and new stimuli. BUT maintains strong relations with embassies, the Institut Français, the Italian Culture Centre, the British Council, the Fulbright Commission and Vision 97 Foundation.

Academic bodies:

- The Academic Senate approves fundamental questions related to the legislation and financial aspects of management. Its legislative duty is to elect the Rector every third year.

- the Board of Trustees consists of 12 members appointed by the Minister of Education. It supervises the management of the property budget and provides strategic orientation for BUT.

- the Scientific Board, the members of which are appointed by the Rector. It deals with promotion procedures for new professorships, and supervises the educational and scientific plan and orientation of creative work at BUT.

The method of data acquisition

An electronic interactive questionnaire was sent to each student of BUT over the internet, together with an explanation of its purpose. Overall, 1 979 students from all faculties answered, of whom 851 were men and 128 were women. For the purpose of this paper the results are aggregated, of course for the inner use of BUT the kind of faculty will be distinguished.

Discussion of the results

Questions and answers can be aggregated to a few logical groups.

Interest in the programme studied: In most cases students chose BUT as their first university after secondary school leaving exam. Enough information about BUT was available during their decision-making. The programme studied was their first choice and it was exactly the one they wanted to study or close to it. Students were satisfied with the programme studied and in case of a new decision they would choose it again.

Interest in the studied programme and its complexity: Most of the students were not currently studying at another university. This could signify that their specific interest was fulfilled with their current studies. But it also calls attention to the complexity of the study required, which demands great attention and concentration. In spite of some lack of clarity in the distribution of answers to a question about time devoted to study, it is clear that learning takes a lot of time.

Difficulty of the programme studied and social background of the students: Most of the students are not employed systematically. This may be due to the difficulty of the particular field of study and the necessity to concentrate on studies. At the same time, it appears that students are not systematically obliged to earn money themselves. In our case study, attention was not paid to the social status of the students. But the results of the 1999 CHES survey show that students gain funds mostly from their parents (92.2%), obtain social benefits (29.7%), obtain scholarships (9.7%), or earn money occasionally (68.5%) or regularly during the year (20.1%).

Contribution of BUT to student satisfaction:

- Learning and teaching conditions and the academic environment are appreciated favourably and very favourably.

- School facilities and student access to them, and the logistic support of the BUT are valued mostly as convenient and very good.

- Students were equivocal about opportunities to consult over personal difficulties with somebody at the university, with responses equally split across "yes" and "rather not" Attention has already been paid to this problem. Eminent teachers have been established as tutors, and first and second year students can consult them. This should create a network of skilled advisors, to whom tutors can, in case of necessity send the students for consultation. In addition, a new Centre for Education and Guidance comprised of three departments (Life-long Learning, Academic Guidance and Third Age University) has been established.

- The CHES survey from the year 1999 produced some data about the different kinds of student problems. The most frequent problems did not concern studies, rather the lack of funds, personal difficulties, difficulties in commuting and in finding alternative accommodation.

- The behaviour of administrative staff towards students appears as rather problematic. It was rated mostly as suitable or not very auspicious. It will be necessary to pay attention to this problem in the future – first of all to detect the reasons in detail and then progressively to remove the problems on both sides.

Humanities subjects:

- The number and structure of these subjects in the curriculum was considered to be satisfactory and even very good by most of the students. But the number of students who viewed it as unsatisfactory was not negligible, and it will be necessary to identify their problems.

- the contribution of studies to language competence was rated predominantly as rather unsatisfactory or satisfactory. This situation was well known and some ways to improvement have been chosen, including discussion with secondary schools, the emphasis laid on using foreign languages in teaching technical subjects, and a move to teaching/learning to the extent of 10% credits in foreign language (for example, lectures involving both lecturers from abroad and teachers from the home university, students' texts in foreign languages, foreign language presentations by students in seminars, and foreign languages diploma papers). The centralisation of foreign languages departments within BUT has been undertaken in order to improve the teaching equipment. The goal of these actions is to reach a situation when students (but not only they) will be able to communicate and to present their ideas in a foreign language.

Partner relations "teacher-student":

- Students answered a question about their preparedness to act as a partner to their teachers in equal proportions "yes" and "I do not know"; a very small number of students said "no". This level of agreement is gratifying. The answers "I do not know" can express both a misunderstanding the question and irresolution or perplexity of students. It would be interesting to know the reasons for the answer "no".

- A question about the willingness of teachers to be partners to students was mostly answered as "some of them", then after a great interval by "almost no teachers", last and in a smaller number by "most of them". As noted earlier, the horizontal relationship "teacher-student" is not yet obvious and it will be necessary to build it up to a more reasonable degree.

The future career of graduates and the contribution of BUT to it: Students predominantly indicated that they had only a rough notion about their future career and that the university partially helped them to create one. Both these results are satisfactory. But this question should be put again, and only to the students at the end of their studies, in their fourth and fifth year. The answers would then be more relevant and would show if the university really cares for the problem and what more could be done.

Interest in any other school activities apart from study: The majority of students cared for these activities from time to time; with a smaller number not interested at all, and a similarly small number indicating they were interested continuously. The students should say what would be interesting and beneficial for them

Student organisations: The majority of students knew about student organisations quite well. When asked if they co-operate with them, most of the students answered negatively. A smaller number co-operated from time to time, with an almost negligible number of regular co-operators. This result is alarming, but not surprising. The CHES survey from the year 1999 yielded similar results.

Conclusions of the case study

The conduct of the case study was favourably accepted by the administration of BUT as well as by the students, who appreciate the possibility of expressing their ideas in this official way.

The results of the case study are not surprising, but nevertheless they are beneficial. They show that:

- Improvement must go on constantly and care for the quality is an everyday task for all.
- The "teacher-student" and "staff-student" relationships need further development, humanities subjects should receive continued attention in study programmes, and the university should follow the future career of graduates.
- It is highly necessary to improve the language competence of students (as well as of teachers and of other staff).
- Co-operation between students and their representative bodies should be improved.
- There is a pressing need to strengthen the feeling of appartenance of students, teachers and staff to the university.

Acknowledgments

The authors would like to thank Mrs. Helena Šebková, Director of the CHES, for her idea to offer the opportunity of preparing this paper and for her everlasting favour.

Thanks are also to be given to Mr. Jan Vrbka, Rector of the BUT, for his permission to realise the case study at this higher education institution and for his support of the project.

The authors are much obliged to Mr. Petr Dub, Vice-rector of the BUT, who took on the burden of organising the case study, for his share in the project and for his effective and valuable help.

Last but not least, thanks are expressed to all students who readily and promptly answered the questions, and to all others who helped to realise this project.

References

The Act No. 111/1998 Coll. on Higher Education Institutions and on Modification and Amendment of Other Acts (The Higher Education Act).

HOLDA. D. (1999),
"The Social Portrait of Higher Education Students in the Czech Republic (III)",CHES, Prague.

Students' Changing Expectations of Higher Education and the Consequences of Mismatches with the Reality

Richard James

This chapter is an initial attempt to make sense of the complexity of changing student expectations and the consequences of these. It focuses on a number of issues involved in understanding and responding to student expectations, including the factors that appear to be affecting them and the educational consequences of mismatches between student expectations and the realities of courses and universities.

Student preferences and expectations, and the relationships of these to institutional expectations and priorities, are exceedingly complex issues for analysis. The complexity is caused in the main part by the highly participatory nature of the higher education enterprise and the two-way interaction between the actions of students and those of universities – the higher education process not only *shapes* student expectations, the education process is itself *influenced* by the character of these expectations.

There is presently no single theoretical framework that adequately deals with these relationships. Students' expectations are as much of their own roles, responsibilities and commitment as they are of universities. Students may develop unrealistically high expectations (for their own levels of achievement, or of university services) or equally may hold narrow or even low expectations (again, of their own capacities and required level of commitment, or of what participating in higher education can offer). Students' expectations pertain to both quality (increasingly captured in "am I getting value for money?") and personal relevance ("is this course really right for me?") and are thus highly diverse and individual in character. To complicate things further, the matching of student expectations against the realities of higher education is played out over both short- and long-term horizons – from satisfaction with the features of the day-to-day experience, such as services, facilities and the in-class experience, through to particular beliefs about the career and life outcomes that course completion might make possible. The lesson here is that simple analyses of student expectations should be treated with suspicion and will be unhelpful in formulating appropriate responses on the part of universities.

The new relationships between students and universities

Over the past few years the Centre for the Study of Higher Education has been conducting research into the decision-making of prospective students, the transition to university, and the quality of the student experience, especially in the first year. This research has been undertaken in a context of a significant change in the relationship between universities and their student communities. This change is evident in the new relationships between higher education and work, the increasingly market-like forms of organisation of higher education, and the new expectations and priorities of students themselves.

Based on our research, student expectations of higher education do seem to be changing. This is most obvious in the declining willingness of many students to engage to the full in university life. CSHE studies (McInnis and James, 1995; McInnis et al., 2000) of first year students across a five year period (1994 to 1999) have revealed a 9% increase in the proportion of full-time students working part-time and surprising increases in the hours students are working. Compared with 1994, fewer students in 1999 reported spending five days a week at university. These empirical findings confirm the experiences of academic staff who feel growing pressure to accommodate student preferences for a more relaxed engagement with the university experience. Students increasingly seek choice – in the subjects to be studied, in delivery modes, in assessment, and in the time spent on campus. Student involvement with university life is subject to new forms of negotiation (McInnis, 2001).

Further evidence of changing student expectations is showing up in the consumer orientation of many students. In recent research conducted for the Australian Universities Teaching Committee project *Assessing Student Learning* (James and McInnis, 2001) we have spoken with academic staff about changing student expectations. Many believe a consumerist pattern of thinking among students, which they believe is a direct result of the expectation that students contribute a greater proportion of the cost of their education, is now emerging during their day-to-day interaction with students. They offer anecdotal reports of students expecting the right to play a more passive role in their learning and, in isolated instances, of students being heard to make direct references to the cost to them of particular course components.

Academic staff are puzzled and worried by what they perceive to be the rapidly changing character of student expectations. Unfortunately, the staff prognosis is often pessimistic. Many believe a greater proportion of students are predominantly instrumental, seek greater spoon-feeding and narrowly reproductive approaches to assessment, and are generally more likely to judge the quality of teaching in terms of "value for money". Staff also believe there is a sharpening distinction between "achievers" and the students who simply wish to do the minimum work to achieve a pass standard, resulting in increasingly bi-modal grade distributions.

Academic staff are especially concerned when student expectations are poorly aligned with their core academic values. Most academic staff have a strong professional commitment to "making a difference", have a clear vision of the educational outcomes they wish to teach towards and the abilities they wish to assess. Many presently feel frustrated in their efforts to do so.

While there is a tendency for academics to conclude that students are seeking effort-free qualifications and threatening the quality of higher education as we once knew it, such a gloomy outlook is probably unjustified – students undertaking part-time employment, for instance, may be earning essential income for meeting the financial costs of undertaking higher education and while doing so they may be developing valuable generic skills as well as opening up graduate career options – and more sophisticated explanations of the nature and origins of student expectations are necessary. Significantly, there are some intriguing inconsistencies between staff impressions of student attitudes and how students' see themselves. CSHE first year research suggests students continue to be highly motivated to learn in their chosen field of study (James et al, 1999; McInnis et al., 2000). Contrary to the narrow vocationalism that is often assumed, students consistently express a strong desire to study in an area of personal interest. There are few indications, in our data based on student self-reports, of any greater instrumentalism or of any new narrowness in student expectations.

Expectations, mismatches and consequences: four ways of looking at the issues

The inconsistencies between the perceptions of staff and students highlight some of the complexity of the operating environment for universities. On the one hand, these differences in perceptions reveal the gulf between the world views of staff and students and how little is known with any certainty about the new nature of student expectations. On the other hand, they highlight the considerable distance we are "at the chalkface" from developing appropriate responses to the new social, economic and technological context of universities.

Academic staff tend to associate changes in student preferences and expectations largely with the emergence of a new consumer-service orientation resulting from the requirement for students to pay a greater proportion of the cost of their education. However, while rising personal costs are certainly a powerful force affecting the character of relationships between teachers and learners, this trend on its own provides insufficient explanation for the ways in which student expectations are changing. The effects of the higher education market and selective entry processes also need to be understood if better sense is to be made of student expectations. Increasingly, vigorous marketing, to the point of "overselling", is affecting student expectations and highly competitive admissions processes are establishing beliefs about personal "success" and "failure" prior to enrolment.

The situation is further complicated by factors beyond the market. The origins of changing student expectations may lie, paradoxically, in the early formative experiences of students on campus. As is argued later, many prospective students hold few concrete expectations of university life before commencement. The first few weeks of enrolment may actually crystallise student expectations and be the first time for some students to give serious thought to what they have undertaken. If the early transition period is highly formative, then the higher education sector should at least consider the possibility that part of the responsibility for the growing detachment of students lies within the sector itself and is related to the less personal and possibly less intensive environment that might be created as a consequence of growing class sizes.

What are the effects of competitive admissions processes on student expectations?

In the United States there have been extensive research programs into college choice (Chapman, 1981; Paulsen, 1990) which have revealed important relationships between college choice processes and the quality of later experiences of higher education (Villella and Hu, 1990; Wiese, 1994). Little research of this kind has been conducted in Australia, however a recent study by the CSHE (James *et al.*, 1999) into student decision-making processes at the entry point to higher education has begun to shed light on the way in which competitive selection processes are shaping student expectations.

Broadly, the findings of the CSHE research suggest many applicants are not in a good position to judge the appropriateness of programs for them or to assess the features of courses overall. Many prospective students base their planning on quite limited, subjective information. We found that many prospective students do not rigorously seek information and their information-seeking skills are often modest. As a consequence, university applicants' draw on chance encounters and questionable sources when shaping their thoughts about suitable courses. Many prospective students seem to work on a superficial set of ideas about curricula being more or less "applied", "analytical", "practical" or "hands on". In most cases, they accept on faith what they are told and are highly susceptible to the serendipity of word-of-mouth testimony.

The principal reason for this situation is that entry scores have come to serve as a proxy for both quality and personal relevance. Prospective students trust the market. Student faith in the likely quality and personal relevance of particular courses is bound up in the selectivity of entry. Thus for most school-leavers the attractiveness of a course at a university increases with the selectiveness of its admissions and students act to maximise the "earnings" from their school results in a largely reputational market. The logic of applicant thinking is summed up by the student who reported "the main reasons [for choosing my preferred course] are the major subjects featured in the course, the university is nearby, and this course has the highest enter of all my preferences".

This situation is well known to school careers advisers and university admissions personnel. One consequence is that faith in competitive admissions acts *against* the development of complex or sophisticated expectations of university while at the same time *raising* the level of expectations. At least for school-leavers, confidence in the market seems to diminish involvement in vigorous information-seeking while also establishing expectations of quality and relevance that are associated with the degree of selectivity of entry. As a result, many students enter higher education with only vague ideas about specific aspects of the experience which lies ahead, yet with considerable confidence that it will be right for them.

There are potentially profound ramifications of mismatches between "quality and relevance" expectations – no matter how vaguely based these may be – and the realities of courses. Clearly, the relationship between competitive admissions and course quality is not at all straightforward – there is little reason why highly selective courses should be those with the best teaching, for instance. Similarly, a relationship between competitive admissions and personal relevance can hardly be assumed.

The research evidence bears out the difficulties in achieving a suitable early "fit" between courses and personal appropriateness. CSHE studies of the first year experience (McInnis and James, 1995; McInnis *et al.*, 2000), have found that one third of first year school-leavers believe, with hindsight, they were not ready to choose a university course during their final year of school. Similarly, Yorke (1999, 2000) identified "wrong choice of programme" as the first among seven key factors in undergraduate non-completion in the United Kingdom.

Perhaps the most vulnerable students in terms of course "fit" are those who are very idealistic about pursuing knowledge for its own sake. Students who were highly committed to learning and academic achievement during their senior secondary education might be seriously dissatisfied or disillusioned if they find their academic success at school has been rewarded with a course they find uninteresting or unchallenging. Yet this disappointment may not reflect any particular problem with the course itself, for the unusually high expectations of some students for an exceptional intellectual experience may be very difficult for universities to meet. In the United States, Wiese (1994) has described the cognitive dissonance that occurs for first year students of this kind when experiences contradict built-up expectations. These students are at particular risk of non-completion, or may adopt instrumental study strategies that severely limit the development of their potential.

This is not to suggest that all students will be unsettled by a university experience that does not match their immediate expectations. The more highly instrumental students (Biggs, 1982), who often enrol in business and engineering fields (James *et. al.*, 1999), may put aside short-term discomfort or dissatisfaction with the university experience in favour of longer term goals. For these students, immediate concerns may be counterbalanced by a desire simply to pass in the long-run.

How do the early experiences of university reshape student expectations?

The transition to university is therefore a particularly significant period for understanding student expectations and their consequences. If competitive selection processes remove the obligation for prospective students to become well-informed, it is not surprising if many students commence higher education with unsophisticated expectations. As a consequence, the early experiences on campus are not only a testing period for expectations but also are likely to be *shaping* new expectations.

The early period at university is known to be a difficult and sometimes disappointing experience for many students. For students who ultimately withdraw from higher education, their decision usually can be traced to the first few weeks of enrolment. Some uncertainty is to be expected with any major life transition, and not all the difficulties in the higher education transition can be traced to unfulfilled expectations or expectation-reality mismatches. Some of the problems of adjustment in the first year arise from difficulties in finding a place within a new peer group, for example. Nevertheless, many of the factors leading to non-completion identified by Yorke (1999, 2000), such as unhappiness with the institutional environment, dissatisfaction with aspects of institutional provision and poor quality of the student experience, are highly suggestive of underlying mismatches of expectations.

The decision to withdraw is the most obvious consequence of students believing their expectations are not being met. A less obvious consequence, and the outcome of a more passive response on the part of students, is simply the "decision" to be less involved in the academic and social life of university. While Australian universities have been successfully strengthening the student adjustment to university life through various first year transition programs (McInnis *et al.*, 2000) we face new challenges in this area. Universities may need to examine the possibility that one reason for the growing detachment of students lies within the sector itself and is related to more impersonal staff-student relationships that are a consequence of growing class sizes. The reality of university for many first year students is large class sizes and limited access to teaching staff. The number of small group teaching opportunities have been reduced in some universities. At the least, it is clear from CSHE research that students have less access to staff for individual attention.

It would be unsurprising if university life appeared to a present day first year student as more impersonal, less embracing and requiring less personal commitment than it did for students of the past. The consequences of this situation are highly speculative, but it is possible that universities are missing the opportunity to "capture" student engagement during the early formative weeks. From the student perspective, it is easy to uncouple from the university experience if the academic and social net allows you to slip through, perhaps more so when the external world offers multiple distractions and opportunities.

The possibility that the early time on campus is actually shaping student expectations, especially in regard to the extent and nature of their involvement and commitment, has not been considered in a serious or systematic way. If we assume that first year students will drift away from university if we allow them to, then there is the significant possibility that universities are implicated in the growing detachment being recognised among undergraduate students. If this is the case, then the solution is clear: work more intensively with students during the first few weeks of the year. The opportunity to disentangle oneself from the university seems to be less of a problem in highly intensive, highly structured academic courses, especially those with small cohorts allowing the development of strong interpersonal rapport between staff and students.

What are the relationships between student expectations, motivation and satisfaction?

It is not possible in this chapter to present a thorough analysis of the relationships between students' expectations and their motivation and satisfaction, yet the possible effects of mismatches of expectations on student motivation and satisfaction are core issues.

One way to begin such an analysis is to use Herzberg's (1993) theory of motivation to work, sometimes known as the hygiene theory or the two-factor theory. Herzberg proposes two sets of environmental factors that affect people's satisfaction and motivation. Hygiene factors, such as the quality of working spaces and amenities, are associated with the level of personal comfort in the workplace. Herzberg argues that the absence of appropriate hygiene factors may cause dissatisfaction, but their presence does not in itself generate a strong commitment. In contrast, motivation factors are those that can inspire a high level of involvement, their presence lifts achievement beyond expectations. Inspiring leadership and intellectually stimulating work are typically thought to be motivation factors. The absence of these does not in itself lead to dissatisfaction, but it does mean that personal involvement will not be raised above mundane levels.

If Herzberg's ideas are applicable to students and their higher education involvement, then a perceived absence of adequate hygiene factors, such as facilities and services, is likely to generate student dissatisfaction, yet the presence of these factors will not on their own lead to satisfaction. To achieve this something of a different order altogether is needed, such as challenging or inspirational experiences that may be surprising and unexpected.

The motivational factors associated with higher education are generally unobservable for outsiders and can only be understood through sustained involvement. As a consequence, student expectations on commencement probably lie closest to hygiene factors. During the process of choice of a course and university, prospective students are known to find it easier to make decisions on course/institution characteristics that lean towards hygiene factors – readily observable, tangible qualities, such as ease of access from home and the ambience of the campus buildings and surroundings (James et al., 1999). However, they have limited access to the less tangible course features that are likely to provide motivation. The less observable dimensions of the university experience are those which capture imagination and spur a continuing commitment, and which are the key to persistence and success at university – these include inspirational teaching and belonging to a thriving peer group and learning community.

Working to meet student expectations of hygiene factors is obviously important, to head off the potential for dissatisfaction, however there are obviously compelling reasons for also giving attention to the factors that motivate students. Curiously, this probably requires consciously creating a degree of mismatch of expectations. Ideally, higher education should provide students with a good deal more than they expected when they enrolled. Ideally, every single student should experience a transformative force at some time during their university experience, something that affects their outlook in significant and predicted ways. Higher education requires challenge to existing thinking that takes students into a state of uncertainty – the realisation of motivation factors may actually require a deliberate confronting of student expectations, with all the tension that might accompany this.

The point to be made here is that for the educational industry, mismatches in expectations are not always harmful. Indeed, they are wholly desirable, being part of the educative process of liberating the minds of students through exposing them to challenge and difference. This is an important reminder, if it were needed, of the risk the present context provides of responding to student expectations by focusing on amenity dimensions of the student experience, which, though very necessary, are ultimately limited elements in making up the overall quality of the university experience.

What is the relationship between student expectations and the quality of higher education?

Since student expectations must have some bearing on their motivation and satisfaction, expectations must in turn influence the quality of higher education for students are co-producers of this quality. The extent to which student expectations or preferences are aligned with the widely agreed goals of higher education and the general consensus on what constitutes quality in higher education is perhaps the ultimate question facing universities.

In one sense, this question can be answered very simply. Students *are* well-equipped to judge the quality of certain aspects of higher education and we should trust their intuitions on these matters. Generally speaking, students are in a reasonable position to judge the more tangible, short-term components of the experience and to judge aspects of the process of higher education. Students can be expected to be reasonable arbiters of the impact on them of the availability of computers, the quality of teaching spaces, the teaching skills of academic staff, and so on. Students have quite straightforward views for the teaching they prefer. They expect the fundamentals of effective teaching – clear goals, feedback on progress, and transparent assessment requirements and grading practices – and they welcome personal interaction with teaching staff and being treated as individuals by staff who show concern for their progress. These expectations thoroughly correspond with what the experts believe generates an effective higher education environment (Ramsden, 1992).

But the student expectation-quality relationship is not altogether this straightforward. Students are not ideally placed to judge other aspects of higher education quality. There are deeper dimensions to quality in higher education, such as the overall coherence of the curriculum, into which students have fewer insights. These aspects of higher education quality are usually less tangible, less intuitive and require a longer term view. Students are not necessarily in the best position to judge these aspects of quality, creating potential clashes between individual student preferences and what is educationally desirable. Students do not necessarily recognise nor welcome the experiences which might lead to educationally valuable outcomes over the long haul.

Needless to say, student expectations alone are not a robust basis for driving educational planning. However, the tensions between educational objectives and student expectations are being played out in a number of curriculum areas and these are the source of day-to-day dilemmas for academic staff. The issues range from the "macro" to the mundane: on the large scale, meeting the new expectations for choice, flexibility and modularity is potentially threatening the careful sequencing of the curriculum that is known to produce the best academic outcomes (Pascarella and Terenzini, 1998). More trivially, academic staff are finding students are questioning their involvement in group activities, yet these activities are often key curriculum elements in the efforts of universities to teach and assess generic skills. Other examples abound – there are, for instance, strident expectations on staff to make lecture notes available on the web prior to lectures, a practice sometimes highly desirable on educational grounds but not always so.

These few examples illustrate the way in which student expectations are impinging on the day-to-day decision-making of academic staff. While some particular points of tension between staff and students may border on the trifling, overall they amount to an indirect and unplanned re-negotiation of the higher education curriculum, fuelled in part by new student preferences and the willingness of students to exert these preferences.

Conclusion: responding through the renewal of the undergraduate curriculum

Students' preferences, expectations and needs have always been intricately interwoven. With an increasing consumerist orientation among students, student preferences are tending to become expectations and meeting expectations is taking on a new importance alongside meeting needs. These changes are significantly affecting the nature of the implicit "deal" between students and the university. Many of the newly emerging expectations appear to be on the "student commitment" side of the ledger. Students expect a more detached association with the university. If unwatched, these expectations have the potential to threaten the quality of education, especially if university responses create more fragmented curricula that provide less coherent educative experiences.

How might universities respond to this situation? First, in a more vigorously competitive market in Australian higher education there is a growing obligation on universities to provide appropriate and accessible information on what they offer. It seems necessary to make more explicit efforts to spell out the experiences that will be provided, the corresponding commitments required on the part of students, and the potential outcomes (James, 2000). Admittedly, this kind of articulation of the university experience is not a simple matter. As we argued in the *Which University?* report, there are limits to which the nature of the university experience can be conveyed prior to becoming part of it – the quality of the experience is only fully understood through living it (James *et al.*, 1999, p. 79). Furthermore, as argued earlier, there are few indications that prospective students are inclined to seek greater amounts of information.

This leads directly to the second point. Student expectations are not set in stone – they can be influenced and better managed by universities. The available evidence suggests that the present university admissions processes do not encourage students to commence higher education with sophisticated understandings of the experience that lies ahead. It follows that efforts to encourage students to develop more complex and sophisticated expectations of university and of their own roles and responsibilities will be valuable. In the first instance, university advertising and information dissemination needs to incorporate a strongly educative dimension. Second, greater efforts are needed to manage expectations during the early formative period of university enrolment. This is the time during which much of the lasting nature of the student-university transaction will be established and universities need to work extremely hard during this period to influence expectations and capture student engagement.

Finally, and perhaps most importantly, we may need to respond to changing student expectations through rethinking the undergraduate curriculum itself. Craig McInnis and myself have recently commenced a long term project to examine the nature of the undergraduate curriculum in Australia. As is obvious to all, the curriculum is groaning under the weight of the expectations held for it. Among other things, student preferences for choice, flexibility and in some cases fast-tracking, the pressure to accommodate the growth in knowledge, and the push to incorporate generic skill acquisition alongside subject specific knowledge have stretched the curriculum to breaking point.

Arguably, the responses of universities to the new pressures on the curriculum have thus far been incremental and piecemeal. What is needed is a systematic new analysis of assumptions about the nature of the undergraduate curriculum and of the university experience overall. Universities need to carve out a new model for the undergraduate curriculum – conceived broadly so as to embrace what is taught, how it is taught, and how learning is assessed – based on sound educational principles and an understanding of the new realities of the social context for higher education. In doing so, universities have an obligation to sort out how to balance new student expectations with the ultimate goal of providing a coherent overall educational experience. The day-to-day character of the student experience may differ markedly from that of the past, particularly now that new forms of interaction with the university are possible, nevertheless the goal of a coherent curriculum experience still provides the justification for determining the point at which, if necessary, a line must be drawn in the sand.

The main tension, as always, lies in providing support and providing challenge and independence. Unfortunately, there is risk that meeting student expectations will become synonomous with lowering the degree of challenge. Already there may be some intersection in the thinking of many academics between the idea of student-centredness, which has become a widespread slogan, and idea of student-as-consumer. Student-centredness brings an emphasis to student needs alongside, or ahead of, institutional/academic priorities. This does not imply, or should not imply, a narrow or thoughtless reactiveness to student expectations. Student-centredness means educators making informed decisions in relation to students' developmental needs and placing the best interests of students at the heart of planning.

References

BIGGS, J. (1982),
"Student Motivation and Study Strategies in University and College of Advanced Education Populations" *Higher Education Research and Development*, 1(1), pp. 33-68.

CHAPMAN, D. (1981),
"A model of student college choice", *Journal of Higher Education*, 52(5), pp. 490-505.

HERZBERG, F., MAUSNER, B. and BLOCH SNYDERMAN, B. (1993),
The motivation to work, Transaction Publishers, New Brunswick, N.J., USA.

JAMES, R. (2000),
"How school-leavers choose a preferred university course and possible effects of the quality of the school-university transition", *Journal of Institutional Research*, 9(1), pp. 78-88.

JAMES, R. and MCINNIS, C. (2001),
Strategically Re-positioning Student Assessment, Discussion paper for the AUTC project "Assessing Student Learning", available at *www.cshe.unimelb.edu.au*

JAMES, R., BALDWIN, G. and MCINNIS, C. (1999),
Which university? The factors influencing the choices of prospective undergraduates, AGPS, Canberra.

MCINNIS, C. (2001),
Signs of disengagement: The changing undergraduate experience in Australian universities, available at *www.cshe.unimelb.edu.au*

MCINNIS, C. and JAMES, R. (1995),
Trends in the First Year Experience in Australian Universities, AGPS, Canberra.

MCINNIS, C., JAMES, R. and HARTLEY, R. (2000),
First Year on Campus: Diversity in the Initial Experiences of Australian Undergraduates, AGPS, Canberra.

PASCARELLA, E. and TERENZINI, P. (1998),
How College Affects Students: Findings and insights form twenty years of research, Jossey Bass, San Francisco.

PAULSEN, M. (1990),
College choice: Understanding student enrolment behaviour, ASHE-ERIC, George Washington University, Washington DC.

RAMSDEN, P. (1992),
Learning to teach in higher education, Routledge, London.

VILLELLA, E.F., and HU, M. (1990),
"College Choice as a Linking Variable Between Recruitment and Retention", *Journal of Marketing for Higher Education*, 3(1), pp. 79-88.

WIESE, M.D. (1994),
    "College Choice Cognitive Dissonance: Managing Student/Institution Fit", *Journal of Marketing for Higher Education*, 5(1), pp. 35-47.

YORKE, M. (1999),
    Leaving Early: Undergraduate Non-completion in the United Kingdom, Falmer Press, London.

YORKE, M. (2000),
    "Smoothing the Transition into Higher Education: What can be learned from student non-completion", *Journal of Institutional Research*, 9(1), pp. 78-88.

83

Encouraging University Responsiveness: Student-focussed Incentives in Australian Higher Education

Michael Gallagher

This chapter covers: general meanings of "responsiveness" and public expressions of it in relation to higher education in Australia; meanings of "responsiveness to varying student needs and circumstances"; government policy objectives and measures; and the responses of universities to the changing structure of incentives.

Meanings of responsiveness

Responsiveness is a characteristic of biological organisms that demonstrate behavioural change when incited by a stimulus. Adaptation to changes in environmental conditions ("learning") is an ecological prerequisite of survival. Responsiveness is the drive to survive. Responsiveness appears to have been predominantly used as a metaphor applied to government expectations of civil institutions in the context of post mid-1970's "oil shock" discussions within the OECD about the "structural adjustment" of industries to fundamental changes in conditions of trade and investment and the applications of technology. In this sense as applied to universities, responsiveness relates to broad social expectations of "adaptability" to change and "contributiveness" to national needs. More recent, market-related meanings of responsiveness as applied to universities include concepts of "competitiveness", "fitness for purpose" and "customer service".

Responsiveness can be both an organisational capability and an external perception. Expectations and perceptions of institutional responsiveness are context, time and purpose dependent. The relativity of responsiveness to context can be seen in the form that policy debates take in other countries, such as universities in Thailand moving from central, input-based financing to devolved, block funding or European states discussing the introduction of student fees. Many features of the Australian higher education system (including institutional autonomy in respect of student admissions, staff hiring, and course design and approval, together with government financing through triennial block funding) are regarded by universities in other nations as more conducive to responsiveness than their own arrangements.

Expectations and perceptions of responsiveness are relative to time and context as reflected in the stage of development of national systems. Far-reaching shifts occurred throughout the 1980s and 1990s in Australia as elsewhere regarding public expectations of government and the scale and role of the public sector. New market-related mechanisms for the supply of services to meet public needs were developed including corporatisation and commercialisation of various public sector agencies, and government relations with public providers were extended to include purchasing of services as well as funding and regulating. Universities were judged by a Federal Government review committee, the Williams Committee, in 1979, to have been reasonably responsive to social needs. In 1988 they were found to be out of touch and in need of fundamental transformation. In 1998, despite the shake-up of the "Dawkins reforms", another federal review committee, the West Committee, saw the need for a radical shift in financing policy. These different views in part reflected assessments of university performance against changing expectations over time.

Timing can be problematic when evaluating responsiveness. On the one hand, "immediate responsiveness" can be an imperative for winning a competitive contract to provide services. In this sense a university, like a consultancy firm, has to be fleet and expedient in organising the best proposal to meet the client's needs. On the other hand, "substantive responsiveness" may take some years to inculcate in the culture and practice of an institution, such as the clarification of graduate attributes and their embedding throughout the curriculum and in teaching and assessment practices. Different people viewing an institution's performance at different points over time may form different opinions on its responsiveness. A commencing student in 2002 may simply take as given the on-line capacities that a university has taken several years and many millions to build, and may even express dissatisfaction with system response times or limited mobility. There is an element of "continuous improvement" implicit in the concept of institutional responsiveness.

The relativity of responsiveness to purpose is complex. Whose purposes take precedence among the many contending demands? Ultimately a university will look to its own long-term interests – its survival in a form that reflects its values. However, it will have to mediate conflicting pressures in so doing, including by being seen to respond reasonably to the requirements and expectations of those on whom its continued existence depends.

The expectations of university clients are reflected in:

- Government planning objectives, targets, priorities, funding initiatives and reporting requirements.

- Industry requirements regarding graduate supply (both quantitative and qualitative).

- Requirements of professional bodies regarding course content and other factors relating to graduates being certified to practise.

- Staff needs, both for attraction and retention, in respect of salaries and conditions of service and access to facilities.

- Business and government service purchase requirements for teaching, research and consultancy services.

- Market opportunities for exploitation of outputs from research and teaching.

- Varying demands of current and prospective students, such as for new course combinations and availability of courses and services in ways and at times convenient to them.

What Maister (1993) calls his "First Law of Service" is also pertinent:

"Satisfaction equals *perception* minus *expectation"*. If the client perceives service at a certain level but expected something more (or different), then he or she will be dissatisfied (Maister, 1993, p. 71).

Referring to professional service firms, Maister comments that a professional may do substantively superior work that is not perceived by the client. Or the professional may invest significant time and effort in dealing with unforeseen contingencies but, because the client did not expect the contingencies, "he or she is irritated by the extra delay and expense rather than thankful for the abilities of the professional". Hence the need to manage client expectations through regular communication.

Maister also points to cultural challenges in ways that may well be applicable to universities:

"The need to be 'client centred' is a constant theme of modern management writings, and it is the professional service sector that is in most urgent need of hearing this message. Because of the proclivity of professionals to become more fascinated with the intellectual challenge of their craft than with being responsive to clients, all too often clients are mocked for their lack of professional knowledge, despised because of their demands, and resented because they control the purse strings and hence the autonomy of the professional" (Maister, 1993, p. 73).

Responsiveness as an organisational capability has structural, procedural and cultural forms. Structural flexibility can be affected by institutional scale and composition, including physical location and technology of provision, breadth of offerings, staffing organisation and access to skill sets – the more "fixed" or "locked-in" are these factors for institutions the lower their response capability. Procedural efficiency requires anticipation and timeliness in decision making, well-developed stakeholder relations and market knowledge, adequate and reliable delivery Systems, sound performance measurement and know how. Cultural readiness involves opportunity-orientation, client-centredness, openness to new views and. approaches, preparedness to take calculated risks and willingness to collaborate. Universities have not been normally designed with such characteristics and therefore face the challenge of having to rebuild themselves in various ways.

Interpretation of developments

The responsiveness theme has had various manifestations in Australian higher education over the last half century. Purposes and emphases have sharpened over time. The following range of meanings of university responsiveness can be gleaned:

- Challenge to academic insularity.
- Compliance with central directives.
- Connection with and contribution to local, regional and national needs.
- Adaptability to change in the operating (competitive) environment.
- Sensitivity to varying student needs and circumstances.
- Readiness to capture global market opportunities.

Initially the universities, and largely for a century of elite access, developed their own modes of responsiveness to student interests and community needs. National imperatives caused government investment and expansion of the system with closer integration of university purposes with the goals of nation building. Massification of participation widened the student body with regard to the diversity of their social backgrounds, the diversity of their aptitude and educational attainment, and the diversity of their needs, interests and motivations. Continuing student demand hit fiscal capacity limits and led progressively to fewer restrictions on universities determining the volume of their enrolments and their tuition prices, except for the bulk of domestic undergraduate students whose fees are set by the Government. The extension of fee-paying access increased student consumer power at a time when universities were becoming more competitive among themselves, and when the interactions of market globalisation with the accelerating power of information and communications technology was opening new markets, developing new products and enabling the entry of new providers.

During the 1990s we have seen in the massified higher education sector a shift from "responsiveness to national needs" as mediated through central planning, resource allocation and regulation (at a time of high university dependency on the state) to "responsiveness to students" as mediating labour market needs through their preferences and choices (during a transition to increasing university self-reliance). At the same time, in the vocational education and training sector, a commensurate shift from central control to user influence has been differently expressed through "responsiveness to industry needs", mediated through a consensus of employer and labour representatives regarding job-related competencies. More recently the universities too have been encouraged to engage more with industry in the learning opportunities they provide for students and through their research. Now at the intersections of these arrangements, and in a more contestable environment for the provision of services, we are seeing new and more integrated forms of expression of student and industry needs, and more innovative ways and means of provider responsiveness.

Generally the universities have traditionally spurned a narrowing of higher education, and especially a short-term, instrumentalist training agenda, notwithstanding that much of their business has traditionally related to preparation for professional employment in applied fields such as medicine, accountancy and engineering. The growth in recent years of student interest in double degree combinations at the undergraduate level perhaps reflects a student-driven desire to cross occupational boundaries in compensation for the narrowness of professional courses and a reaction to the Australian tendency for early specialisation. The key provider-led change has been the clearer definition of "graduate attributes" in the higher education sector, integrating academic and performative learning objectives and the deliberate efforts by the leading institutions to embed them in curricula, teaching and assessment. Within an increasingly competitive environment those universities that can best accommodate diverse student interests and employment-relevant offerings are most likely to prosper.

Similarly, those institutions likely to benefit from the new structure of incentives for research and research training are those that focus on what they do best and give effective attention to the needs of their research students, enable them to undertake research relevant to their interests and aspirations, provide opportunities for them to broaden their skills and understandings as well as deepen their knowledge, and facilitate their timely completion of research training with sound supervision in a quality research environment. Student completions account for 50% of the formula for allocating fully-subsidised research student places. In effect, those institutions who best serve their students will be best rewarded and students will have opportunities to do their research training in the best performing universities in particular areas of research.

Government objectives, initiatives and measures

The Australian Government's stated objectives (Kemp, 2001) for its higher education policies are to:

- Expand opportunity.
- Assure quality.

- Improve universities' responsiveness to varying student needs and industry requirements.

- Advance the knowledge base and university contributions to national innovation.

- Ensure public accountability for the cost-effective use of public resources.

Incentives for universities to respond to student needs

Today's universities are having to respond increasingly to market needs, through the expression of student preferences as to what, where, when and how to study, and their service expectations. While particular services that universities can offer, such as research and consulting services, are potentially expanding market opportunities and are being purchased increasingly by businesses and government agencies, student consumer power is becoming the dominant driver of developments. However, Australia's higher education system is still in a period of transition towards a more market-driven structure of provision. During this transition, shifts in the structure of incentives as established by the Government have particular potency.

The structured incentives that Government has put in place for encouraging university responsiveness to student needs include: 1) negotiated, general-purpose government funding; 2) stipulated government funding; 3) performance-based government funding, including competitive tendering; 4) public accountability reporting; 5) student financing; and 6) quality assurance and consumer protection. The present combination of incentives is the product of a long period of policy evolution which is itself not typically a linear nor coherent process. At any stage the policy framework is under review in order to smooth out internal anomalies or accommodate change in the external environment. So it is possible that mixed signals are received by universities from time to time and that their response strategies may need to be varied or at least allow for contingencies.

Even within a consistent rhetoric of policy intent, such as "selectivity and concentration" in research, key incentives may be altered. A couple of universities, for instance, that responded vigorously to the opening of access to research grants and funding for research training in the early 1990s found themselves in a relatively difficult position with the addition of performance measures to the allocation of research training places a decade later. Even though advance notice was given of the changed incentives, through both an extended period of consultation and phased implementation, the nature of the change stretched the ability of some to "turnaround".

General government funding

Funding of planned enrolments by field and level. The bulk of Commonwealth funding is provided in the form a single block operating grant for teaching-related purposes.

Funding is allocated to universities at normative prices for student enrolments, weighted by field and level of study, A "total student load target" and an "undergraduate load target" are set through negotiation and approved by the Minister. If a university consistently under-enrols below the agreed targets it may subsequently forfeit some funding or be required to compensate in later years by "re-instating" the places. If the university offers fee-paying undergraduate places the penalties for under-enrolment against the targets are automatic and at a set funding rate per place.

The *policy intent* is to give universities flexibility in determining their mix of course offerings and student enrolments in accordance with their mission objectives and their own strategies. The *policy impact* has been a reasonable equilibrium between graduate supply and labour market absorption as measured by graduate employment and earnings. Some over-supply of places relative to student demand is apparent for agriculture, science and engineering. Some under-supply is apparent for health and veterinary science (Li *et al.*, 2001, p. 20).

Marginal funding for undergraduate over-enrolment. Where a university meets its total load target and over-enrols against its undergraduate target it may be paid for the additional undergraduate places at a discounted rate (A$ 2 640 in 2001) as compared with the average funding rate per undergraduate place of A$ 10 300. Each university can determine any level of over-enrolment consistent with its assessment of demand and capacity and its commitment to quality assurance.

The *policy intent* is to encourage resource utilisation efficiency and to give some benefit to institutions that use their capacity at the margin to accommodate additional students. The *policy impact* has been mixed. While some universities have managed the additional flexibility to accommodate changes in demand, others have over-enrolled beyond their marginal capacity and are spending much more per additional place than they receive for these extra places.

Targeted Government funding

Competitive tendering for innovation in provision of places to meet skill shortages. In January 2001 a set of initiatives to foster national innovation was announced in the *Backing Australia's Ability* package. Funding was provided for an extra 2000 student places. For the first time universities were invited to bid against a set of criteria to provide places in mathematics, science and technology and related fields for a fixed price per student place. Competitive bids were assessed for their strength, fitness to demand and innovativeness in curriculum and delivery. The winning universities have to sign up to "additionality" agreements and their delivery against their tender specifications will be evaluated in subsequent years with a view to determining whether any places should be re-allocated.

The *policy intent* is to encourage more innovative educational offerings that are more relevant to the competitive needs of Australian businesses. The *policy impact* so far has been the development of new courses and innovations in course design and delivery consistent with the need to prepare graduates with appropriate skill sets.

Regional places. The 2001-02 Budget provided funding for an extra 670 places targeted to demographically-growing regions with relatively low rates of higher education access and participation. For one region, Geraldton, as a trial of an option for allocating growth, tenders have been invited from all universities to serve community needs.

The *policy intent* is to increase regional access to higher education. The *policy impact* cannot yet be evaluated. However, new forms of regional provision are emerging, to which this initiative contributes. The new forms include multi-sector institutions (composite university and Technical and Further Education – TAFE – providers), multi-sector precincts (single campus administration, articulated courses offered and quality-assured by parent providers, including a university, a TAFE college and a State and/or private secondary school), course articulation agreements, where graduates from TAFE or other VET providers are given credit recognition for university awards; "hub and spoke" university services incorporating a mix of contact and virtual delivery through "learning centres" or "telecottages"; and fully on-line service provision.

Higher Education Innovation grants. An annual program of grants is available for supporting innovation and collaboration in the development and provision of courses, such as collaborative provision in fields of low enrolment, innovative projects in science-related education, and projects to enable university access to information and communications technology.

The *policy intent* is to encourage innovation and diffuse best practice. The *policy impact* appears to be both increased speed and spread of innovation.

Capital Development Pool. An annual program of grants is available for specific capital works. The program emerged as the residual element following the capital roll-in after the growth surge in funded enrolments in the early 1990s. It has been directed to supporting campus development in new areas and, increasingly to encourage collaboration among universities and TAFE colleges, and investment in electronic delivery technology.

The *policy intent* is to support changes in demographically-driven demand. The *policy impact* is demonstrated by increasing university-TAFE collaboration and use of electronic delivery.

Workplace Reform Program. Universities were offered a supplement of 2% of their operating grants as a further contribution to the salaries cost outcome of enterprise bargaining. Conditions were attached to the funding for the purpose of encouraging flexibility in management, administrative and industrial arrangements.

The *policy intent* is to increase university responsiveness to student, industry and community needs. The *policy impact* is reflected in enterprise agreements that provide increased management flexibility.

Teaching development grants. An annual program of grants is allocated on the advice of the Australian Universities Teaching Committee. The grants have supported individual and institutional projects and some collaborative projects. Recent emphasis has been given to examining curriculum and learning outcomes in particular fields of study and on general themes such as teaching large classes. Information about projects and developments is widely disseminated.

The *policy intent* is to raise the status of teaching and to improve teaching practice. The *policy impact* is reflected in increasing levels of graduate satisfaction with university teaching.

Australian awards for university teaching. National awards are presented annually to individuals and teams of university teachers by field and to institutions for their services to students and their communities.

The *policy intent* is to raise the status of teaching, recognise and disseminate good practice. The *policy impact* is reflected in greater attention by universities to teaching skills development of staff and teaching performance as a consideration in promotions.

Performance-based funding

Performance-based funding for research training places. Funding for tuition-free research student places has been separated from operating grants for teaching-related purposes and allocated each semester, from 2001, through a performance formula weighted 50% for completions (domestic and on-shore international graduates), 30% research income and 10% research output.

The *policy intent* is to improve the quality of research supervision and research training environments, to improve student completion rates and times, and to better relate research training to the needs and destinations of graduates. The *policy impact* has been strong and immediate, as is evident through the revised strategies of universities for intake of research students, a sharper focus on areas of research strength and greater attention to the selection, training and monitoring of supervisors.

Performance-based funding for research infrastructure. Funding for general research-related infrastructure is allocated via a formula weighted 60% research income (all sources of income treated equally), 30% domestic research student load (with high-cost places 2.35 times low-cost places) and 10% research output (with books five times the value of other outputs). From 2003 the output measures will include patents, refereed designs and exhibited works.

The *policy intent* is to support research excellence. The *policy impact* is a concentration of resources in the best performing areas.

Equity and indigenous support funding. Support funds for equity target groups and indigenous students are allocated annually on a performance basis according to student access, retention and success rates.

The *policy intent* is to achieve higher levels of participation and better outcomes for equity groups. The *policy impact* has been strong on increasing access but the relatively low incentive payments have not led to significant improvements in progression and completion.

Planning and accountability monitoring and performance reporting

Educational profiles strategic documentation. As a condition of operating grant funding the Minister may require universities to furnish planning documentation, data and reports. The present set of requirements includes a strategic plan; an educational profile of enrolments; a capital management plan; a quality improvement plan; an equity plan; and a plan for indigenous students. In 2001 a census of units of study is being conducted to identify the extent of web-enhanced and on-line provision. The Government has encouraged universities to specify the "attributes" they aim for their graduates to have developed.

The *policy intent* is partly to guide resource allocation decisions and for public accountability reporting, and also to promote strategic improvement in university management. The *policy impact* is evidenced by improved institutional planning and reporting.

Research and Research Training Management Reports (RRTMR). In addition to the above set of plans the RRTMR, introduced as part of the reforms announced in the 1999 White Paper, *Knowledge and Innovation*, requires universities to identify their research objectives and strengths, the outputs of research active staff, their IP management policies, the profile of their research students by field in relation to strengths, their policies for research supervision, and their performance in relation to their objectives.

The *policy intent* is to improve Australia's research performance by concentrating resources on areas of strength, to increase the utilisation of research, including for commercial exploitation, to improve the quality of the research training experience and to improve completion rates and times. The *policy impact* has been strong and fast (mainly because of linkages to the formula-based research funding incentives above) especially on internal priority setting by universities.

Graduate Destinations and Satisfaction monitoring. The quality improvement plans and the RRTMRs have some mandatory elements – graduate destinations and satisfaction for the former, and graduate satisfaction for the latter. A national survey of graduates is conducted annually by the Graduate Careers Council of Australia, tracing employment destinations and starting salaries. A national instrument, the Course Experience Questionnaire (and an equivalent instrument for Postgraduates) is used annually to obtain measures of graduate satisfaction with their overall experience, teaching and generic skills formation. A Graduate Skills Assessment instrument has also been developed for institutions, graduates and employers to use to verify the attributes that graduates are expected to possess.

The *policy intent* is to have public comparisons of institutional performance as perceived by graduates as an incentive for continuous improvement of universities. The *policy impact* is mixed in the context of variable response rates, signs of student "survey fatigue" and a lack of consensus within the system as to the validity and reliability of such instruments.

Diversity characteristics and performance indicators. The Department publishes regularly, and maintains on its web site trend data for, various sets of comparative institutional performance indicators, including a web-based site for prospective students that relates to ten fields of study.

The *policy intent* is to inform the community and institutions themselves about relative performance in a diverse system. The *policy impact* interacts with peer pressure and competition. With a large number of institutions and indicators it is possible for each university to construct a set that reflects best on it. Institution-wide indicators have limited influence of student choice, which appears to be informed by field of study.

Student-financing incentives

Access through fee-paying. Overseas and domestic students can access higher education through direct payment of fees to universities. The universities can determine the volume of their enrolments and their prices in respect of overseas students (so long as the floor price recovers costs), postgraduate students (by coursework and research), and undergraduate students (except that institutions with publicly-subsidised students can enrol undergraduate fee-payers only up to 25% of enrolments in a course).

The *policy intent* is to widen access and choice, and increase consumer pressure on universities to respond to community needs. The *policy impact* has been very strong for many but not all universities, as reflected in the wide variation in fee-paying enrolments across institutions. Universities report that fee-paying students are increasingly demanding in their expectations of service.

Access with Government assistance. Domestic students at universities listed on the tables of the *Higher Education Funding* Act can access an income-contingent deferred payment loan (HECS) to the level of the fee set by the Government for the course of their choice. From 2002, postgraduate coursework students at those universities

95

will have access to a similar income contingent loan to meet fees set by universities. Students enrolled with Open Learning Australia, for undergraduate studies, also have access to a HECS-style loan, so long as they maintain a minimum study load for fees set by the Government; however, OLA can charge above the Government basic rate and students pay the gap directly through fees.

The *policy intent* is to enable equitable access and require the direct beneficiaries to pay a share of the costs. The *policy impact* has been powerful, as evidenced by strong growth in demand for HECS places. The deferred repayment option possibly dampens student consciousness of costs.

Quality assurance, international openness and consumer protection

Quality assurance framework national protocols. Australian universities as self-accrediting institutions established by statute are responsible for ensuring their academic standards. The Commonwealth and State and Territory governments have agreed a set of national protocols that require universities to be established only by statute, protect the business name of university, require all other providers to be accredited and monitored by the State or Territory accrediting authority, and require monitoring of delivery arrangements involving other organisations, the operation of overseas higher education institutions in Australia and the endorsement of higher education courses for overseas students. Overseas students enrolled in registered Australian institutions have consumer protection rights through the *Education Services for Overseas Students* Act. The ESOS Assurance Fund addresses the problem of college collapses which have previously disrupted student studies and threatened the loss of their pre-paid fees. Unless exempted, providers of education and training to overseas students must contribute to the Assurance Fund. The quality assurance processes of universities and accrediting bodies are to be audited over a five-year cycle by an independent Australian Universities Quality Agency. Reports of audits will be made public and follow-up action by universities and other providers will be assessed by the responsible government.

The *policy intent* is to assure the quality of Australian higher education to students and the community, to underpin the competitiveness of Australian universities overseas, to prevent the operations of providers that do not meet required standards, and to protect students as consumers. The *policy impact* has been strong on those few providers found to be operating without meeting standards. The more competitive environment, performance reporting requirements and the external audit cycle are requiring universities to maintain their attention to matters of quality.

General Agreement on Trade in Services commitment. Australia is one of the few World Trade Organisation members to make "education services" commitments under the General Agreement on Trade in Services. One of Australia's commitments places "no limitations" on market access for the provision of private university level education services. The commitment provides a competitive stimulus to institutions with flow on benefits to students.

The *policy intent* is to widen student choice and expand opportunities for Australia's universities overseas. The *policy impact* is reflected in Australia's relatively high share of the world trade in education.

University responses

In broad terms the higher education system has responded reasonably well, albeit somewhat slowly, to the various incentives. It appears to be responding more quickly in the context of increasing competition and direct pressure from students. Even the more recent policy initiatives, especially the reforms to research and research training, are having immediate impacts on university planning and practice.

Total student enrolments have grown by 210 419 or 43% over the period 1990 to 2000. Overseas students, either paying fees or funded through aid programs and drawn from 207 countries, have trebled over the same period to 95 607, representing one third of the overall increase in student numbers. Fee-paying student (full-time equivalent) enrolments represent one quarter of total enrolments in 2001, including both domestic and overseas students. The fee-paying share of Australian student enrolments has increased from less than 3% in 1992 to over 10% in 2001. The share of total fee-paying enrolments (including off-shore) varies across universities from 5% to 44%.

There has been a shift to external student enrolment over the decade of some 3 percentage points and a corresponding decline in the proportion of full-time students. Over the same period there was growth in the student body aged 20 through to 30 years from 30% to 38% of all students, and a corresponding decline by some 7 percentage points in the younger, direct from school age cohort. Admissions direct from school have fallen from 59% in 1990 to 56% in 2000, while admissions from TAFE have risen from 3% to 7%. Overall there has been a modest widening of university admissions.

Whereas all non-overseas students grew by 18.8% over the period 1991-2000, enrolments of indigenous students grew from a very low base by 60%, students from low socio-economic backgrounds by 25%, and students from rural and isolated communities by 19%. Massification of higher education appears not to have been exclusively to middle-class advantage. Some refinement of socio-economic indicators is required and is underway, in view of problems associated with the reliance on postcode data. Changes in enrolments of students from non-English-speaking backgrounds largely reflect shifts in immigration policy. Achievements for women in non-traditional areas whilst impressive need to be interpreted in the context of increasing feminisation of the higher education student body.

These significant shifts in commencing enrolments variously across levels and fields suggest a higher education system that is reasonably responsive to labour market needs as expressed through student choices.

Exploring the relationship between student applications, university offers and enrolments over 1992 to 1999, Li *et al.* (2000) found a complicated picture but one that supports the view that Australian universities are responsive to student demand to some extent. They are most responsive to school leaver demand and accommodate the balance of their enrolments to meet government targets through their acceptance of direct applications:

> "When we took account of movements in enrolments we found that the supply of offers was directly related to the demand for places. Universities were responsive at this level. For every additional 100 applications through the admission centres there will be an additional 84 offers. It also appears that the majority of additional places provided by Government go to those who apply through the admission centres (mostly school leavers). For every additional 100 enrolments an additional 150 offers are made. What appears to be the case is that direct new enrolments are the 'swing' variable, which universities use to meet the aspirations of those who apply through admission centres and the requirements of Government."

Li *et al.* (2000) also found some evidence of university responsiveness to shifting student demand by field of study. However, they also found some stickiness that may reflect staffing and infrastructure inflexibilities which constrain quickness of response. Several matters warrant more detailed investigation.

Universities have been striving to increase their staffing flexibility over time, though at a slower rate than for the economy overall. Full-time staff comprised 82% of all staff in 1991, falling to 75% in 2000, while casual staff rose over the decade from 10% to 15%.

The composition of staff also changed, with some "hollowing-out" of the lecturer and senior lecturer levels. Growth occurred at the below lecturer and above senior lecturer levels, the latter possibly reflecting traditional promotion practices.

One consequence of the apparent imbalance between university responsiveness to student demand and internal rigidities has been some upwards movement in student:staff ratios (SSR). These shifts have not been uniform, either across academic organisation units, or among universities. Clearly there are institution-specific explanations for these variations.

A related matter that warrants further investigation is that of very small student enrolments in units of study. Some 20 656 units, 23% of the total, are recorded as having fewer than five students enrolled in 2000. There are some coding issues with these data which would tend to exaggerate the apparent problem; however, it appears there is scope for efficiency improvement that may enable several institutions to better accommodate student numbers, and reduce SSRs, in the larger units.

There is also wastage associated with poor retention, progression and completion rates for students in some institutions in some fields. Martin *et al.* (2001a) find that only 64% of the cohort of commencing undergraduate students in 1992 completed an award at the university where they enrolled by 1999, and estimate a final completion rate of 71.6% for that cohort. For the 1993 cohort, the final completion rate is estimated at 70.8%. Martin *et al.* (2001b) report that by 1999, 53% of postgraduate research doctoral students and 31% of masters students who commenced an award course in 1992 had completed that course. They estimate the final completion rates of the cohort to be 65% for doctoral and 48% for masters students. They also found that "university specific factors explain a significant proportion of the variation in completion rates".

The universities generally are responding positively and genuinely to the need to give more and better attention to their students, reinforced by government incentives to do so and by competitive pressures. There also have been many advances in curriculum design, more flexible provision of courses and combinations of courses, and improvements to teaching and assessment practices across the system. There is a discernible shift in the valuing and professionalising of teaching and a stronger focus on learning outcomes. Substantial investments have been made in the design and development of sophisticated online materials, units of study, interactive learning experiences and student support services. The best in this regard are leading world practice. Several universities are now more actively engaging with their regional communities educationally, culturally and economically.

However, there are further challenges ahead. Dunkin and Lindsay (2000) contrast the assumptions that traditionally underpin curriculum design for a cohort of students commencing higher education direct from school with those relevant to a cohort of lifelong learners:

"In designing our teaching and learning programs we tend to assume that:

- The target audience are school leavers with minimal life experience and a high need for structure and guided learning.

- This group needs an initial post-secondary qualification to begin a career.

- The students are full-time and/or available to attend campus-based instruction.

- Programs should reflect professional/vocational or disciplinary specialisations.

- Academic staff provide the gateway to knowledge expertise and their role is to disseminate this knowledge.

Yet those who pursue lifelong learning are commonly:

- Working adults who are accustomed to managing themselves in work or life; forced to juggle competing demands for their time and their resources.

- Increasingly seeking updated or further formal education to support their career, and the frequent and lateral moves that are now open to them.

- Facing problems at work that are multifaceted and require systemic or team-based solutions/approaches.

- Able to access knowledge/information through several different avenues."

Dunkin and Lindsay point to some of the implications of this shift in the student population, including the need for new ways of teaching and learning, the application of adult learning theory that calls for a wider range of learning experiences (and respect for and recognition of the prior experiences of students), and the tailoring of courses to meet the needs of paying customers.

A new set of expectations of university responsiveness, now driven more directly by students themselves, is rapidly emerging. The responsiveness of universities so far to the set of incentives of recent years positions them in many ways to accommodate the new demands. The competitive pressures of the future are likely to urge increasing responsiveness.

References

DUNKIN, R. and LINDSAY, A. (2001),
"Universities as Centres for Lifelong Learning", in D. Aspin, J. Chapman, M. Hatton and Y. Sawano (eds), *International Handbook of Lifelong Learning Part Two*, Kluwer Academic Publishers, London.

KEMP, D. (1999),
Knowledge and Innovation: a policy statement on research and research training, AusInfo, Canberra.

KEMP, D. (2001),
Higher Education Report for the 2001 to 2003 Triennium, DETYA. Canberra.

LI, J., KARMEL, T. and MACLACHLAN, M. (2000),
Responsiveness – Do universities respond to student demand? Occasional Paper Series 00/F, Higher Education Division, DETYA, Canberra.

MAISTER, D. (1993),
Managing The Professional Service Firm, Simon and Schuster, New York.

MARTIN, Y.M., MACLACHLAN, M. and KARMEL, T. (2001a),
Undergraduate Completion Rates: An Update, Higher Education Division, DETYA, Canberra.

MARTIN, Y.M., MACLACHLAN, M. and KARMEL, T. (2001b),
Postgraduate completion rates, Higher Education Division, DETYA, Canberra.

Marketing in Higher Education: Matching Promises and Reality to Expectations

Sarah Davies

Introduction

This chapter looks at the nature of marketing in Australian universities, it examines what we know about student expectations and looks at issues of definition. How should we define students: are they consumers, customers, or stakeholders, and what are the differences and implications?

Putting marketing and student expectations together, what role does marketing play in creating and then managing the expectations and perceptions of students, and what could university marketers do to try to resolve or move on from the tensions around the "students as customers" debate?

The role and nature of marketing in higher education

The policies and actions of recent and current state and federal governments in Australia have created an environment of intense competition among tertiary institutions. These policies and funding arrangements have created a set of behaviours and attitudes in tertiary marketers which mirror those of the commercial, for-profit world. All tertiary institutions now have very professional, comprehensive marketing functions and take the competition very seriously, and Australia has developed an international reputation for being quite aggressive in its marketing and recruitment practices.

Economic reality forces Australian universities to compete hard for students, research funding, industry sponsorship and consulting. From a marketing perspective, where this results in increased accountability and professionalism, it is a much needed, powerful incentive to improve performance and ensure we deliver on our promises.

However, where it results in marketing activities which are considered inappropriate for public education providers, we are in danger of adopting behaviour which may be detrimental to our organisations and to the learners and communities we serve.

There are numerous definitions of marketing:

- Human activity directed at satisfying needs and wants through exchange processes (Kotler *et al.*, 1989, p. 4).

- Achieving organisational goals by determining the needs and wants of target markets and delivering the desired results more effectively and efficiently than competitors (Kotler *et al.*, 1989, p. 15).

- To create and keep customers at a profit (anyone who is a shareholder!).

What is important to remember is that marketing is about achieving the objectives of the university through understanding what our potential students need and want. Nowhere is it stipulated that students will know what all their needs are, or that they will be able to articulate them.

What is marketing in a university?

So what is the role and nature of marketing in higher education? It can be argued that courses, programs and qualifications are products, but that they are delivered with all the characteristics of services. Therefore services marketing methods are often deemed most relevant.

Education marketers often refer to the generic challenges of services marketing:

- *Intangibility* – where you are purchasing an abstract, a "performance" – where the value for the student lies in the new levels of understanding and performance which have transformed them.

- *Inseparability* – where, for learning to take place, there needs to be a willing and active student and an effective teacher coming together at the same time, and an underlying support service contract.

- *Perishability* – an empty class cannot be saved or preserved – it is a lost opportunity.

- *Heterogeneity* – the challenge of delivering consistent quality.

What is interesting is that with the growth of non-traditional methods of delivery, some of these challenges become less relevant. Through virtual campuses and electronic communication groups there does not have to be the simultaneous face-to-face coming together of learner and teacher (inseparability). With self-paced learning methodologies, email, bulletin boards, or study guides, the learning experience can be preserved for other times and places (perishability). And with on-line teaching it is easier to achieve standardisation and quality control (heterogeneity).

The challenge that still exists is intangibility. Walshe (2001) asks "How many other organisations can you think of that ask their customers for thousands of dollars in advance, coupled with thousands of hours of significant personal effort, all with no sure knowledge of how they are going to benefit at some unknown stage in the future?"

Not all services marketing methods are easily transferable to education. There are significant limitations to the scope of marketing in higher education:

- No input on price. Most undergraduate students in Australia incur debts which are repaid to the government through the tax system, but do not pay fees to the university. Even with fee for service products, marketers are rarely invited to develop proper pricing strategies. Not only is this a waste of the talent and opportunity on offer from professional marketers, it is also increasingly dangerous as the Australian Competition and Consumer Commission has clearly put universities in its sights in relation to issues like pricing and advertising.

- No input into product. If there were a good relationship between the marketing staff and academics, marketers might be invited to provide comment on what sort of courses students are asking for, what they think will be areas of high demand, what courses do not seem to be attracting the numbers. However, program focus and content definitely belong in the world of the academic.

- No input into place/distribution/convenience. Again, marketers may be asked for their opinion of how and when a program should be delivered, but such matters are determined by academics.

- Little relationship with the student once they become enrolled. Traditionally, marketers have only focussed on bringing prospective students to the university. Marketers are not responsible for managing the relationship, or the experience, with the students once they start their studies. Sometimes, depending on the organisation structure, marketers pick up the responsibility again at the other end when students become alumni, but we leave them in the middle.

The last three factors, in particular, have significant impact on the role of marketing in relation to matching promises and reality to expectations, especially as all university marketers are now, to varying degrees, developing brand building and management strategies for their institutions.

Brand management in a university

Cartwright and Young (1999) argue that the need to market higher education runs counter to educators' professional norms which assert that students are not customers and student learning is not a product to be marketed: "we will teach and they will come".

In higher education, the concept of having a "brand" to be managed is relatively new and in some instances not well understood or accepted. Issues such as the commoditisation of education and the over commercialisation of education get brought into the debate. Marketing principles are very well accepted when seen in terms of student recruitment and publicity, but are generally seen as less critical in terms of investing in brand management and positioning.

Technically a brand is a trademark or name that identifies a product as belonging to a particular manufacturer or distributor. The communication or presentation of a brand in the market place is designed to portray specific characteristics of that product in order to elicit both an emotional and intellectual response in the target market. On a simple level, this is normally a response which results in a sale as well as reinforcing the value of the brand to those who already have purchased the product. For education, brand awareness and respect supports the recruitment of new students. It also supports alumni through continuing to demonstrate that their qualification is respected and valued in the market.

If we can substitute the word "brand" with "trust mark", it begins to have more of an accepted legitimacy in the educational context.

Despite significant pockets of discomfort among some academic communities, universities are increasingly taking a strategic approach to marketing. When developing a brand campaign it is critical to understand the brand attributes as perceived by the target markets. First identify what the brand means to consumers (what they think and feel about the brand). The future of the brand direction is obviously determined by the strategic objectives and goals of the organisation. It is then a journey from where the brand is in the minds of existing markets to where the organisation wants it to be in the minds of its future target markets.

This is brand management, or reputation management; building and creating the desired reputation in the minds of those we seek to influence which in turn leads them to behave in particular ways (for example, undertaking study, awarding a consulting contract, awarding a research grant, or accepting an offer of employment).

Successful brand management is clearly dependent on delivering all the "promises" made about the brand (such as best employment opportunities for graduates, best understanding of industry needs and best capability of meeting those needs, best research facilities, or a challenging and rewarding work environment). Even though there will always be an element of pushing an organisation's performance boundaries through brand presentation, the reality must match the rhetoric.

The dangers of false representation through brand promises are obvious. It is extremely difficult to recover from losing credibility in a market. Any marketing or branding expenditure is wasted if the target audience does not see it as being authentic.

As well as delivering on brand promises, it is important that the university, which the brand has to represent and articulate, is closely attuned to market needs and capabilities. If the university is not responding to market needs and circumstances, then there is a danger that the brand or image will reflect market needs but not be true to organisational capability and goals. This will result in false promises – where the university does not want to or cannot fulfil the expectations being promulgated by the marketing messages. If, conversely, the brand is communicating the organisational goals then it will not be relevant to the target markets. This will result in lack of interest in what the university is offering from the potential students.

If this is what university marketers should be doing, how are we performing? Many of the branding and positioning messages and campaigns used by tertiary institutions are descriptive and feature-based and are easily interchangeable.

In addition, the communication channels used to deliver these messages to the target audiences are very crowded. We are all claiming the same "unique" features and benefits (innovative, international, high graduate employment, real world) in media cluttered with almost identical messages from other institutions. Once again, the problem seems to lie in our inability to differentiate adequately.

Michael Porter identified differentiation as one of three generic strategies leading to sustainable competitive advantage (the others being cost leadership and focus). A university following this strategy is one where its courses, teaching and learning approaches, and research activity are significantly distinct, valued by students (customers) and protected from competitive imitation.

The danger is that when we cannot legitimately differentiate, we are tempted to make statements and promises that are unauthentic and that we may not be able to keep. Whilst we may make these promises to try to make our institution's message stand out from the crowd, they inevitably affect potential student expectations.

Universities in Australia are positioning themselves towards the perceived needs of their markets and against the perceived inadequacies of other institutions. All seek to claim different market segments. All use sophisticated advertising and promotion tools and are looking to create an unambiguous image and brand. All focus on the trading potential of qualifications, against their exchange value in the job market. We live in a world of consumer guides, rankings, and best-buy comparisons.

The pendulum between, on the one hand, commercial and "breaking through the noise" marketing approaches and on the other, the values of being public education providers of scholarship and learning, is in danger of swinging too far towards the former. If this continues, the inevitable outcome will be that the market will no longer listen to or believe our messages and students will be dissatisfied with what they experience compared with what we lead them to expect.

Students/customers

Some fundamental questions for university marketers:

- What is the product – a service, a course, the graduating student, the learning process?

- Who is the consumer – the government, the employer, the learner, the community?

- What is the "student" – a student, a customer, a stakeholder, all of the above? And depending on the answer, what are the various needs, expectations, behaviours and responsibilities?

There are very few industries where marketers and the organisations they work for, are unsure of the answers to these questions! You have to ask what sort of marketer is able to put together a cohesive, effective marketing strategy in this environment?

The current climate suggests that students should be seen (partially if not fully) as customers. They are increasingly aware of their rights and have specific expectations and demands. Sander *et al.* (2000) argue that "education has typically adopted an 'inside out' approach, with those on the inside assuming that they know what students need and what they expect the teacher to give. However, successful service industries have been shown to think 'outside in'. They research what customers expect of the service and then work to provide the service that meets those customer expectations."

The criticism often made by marketers of education is that some academics seem to develop and deliver their programs based only on their intellectual property resources. This is like a manufacturing organisation making a particular product just because they have the machinery to make it. Walshe (2001) comments that marketers have been directed to "put every effort into selling the products we churn off the assembly line. This transactional approach does not represent a strategic approach to the competitive environment and undermines the potential contribution of marketing to an institution's success".

What we must be wary of, however, is a reactive and superficial response to external market needs. We must help the external community to recognise and acknowledge the academics' role as "senior learners". Universities must lead thought and knowledge development. This is widely accepted in a research context and equally valid in a curriculum and program context. Even in the most commercial environment, no professional marketer will advocate that the customer must be the only one to drive product design and innovation. There are plenty of commercial examples where this approach has led to spectacular failures (for example, Coke and Coke Classic).

Universities need to find this balance between developing a market orientation and understanding and managing student expectations. They need to look after customer needs and, where appropriate, subtly re-engineer them. Research on student expectations of higher education shows that expectations of service quality change over time and are dependent on a number of factors both personal to the student and as determined by their broader environment and experiences.

Scott (1999) argues that the "reluctance of professionals to embrace marketing appears to be a fear of a power shift toward the student, as encapsulated in the adage that the 'customer is always right'".

This fear that you do whatever you have to do to make the customer happy, based on their expectations, has led some to conclude that "the concepts of student and customer are in conflict" (Scott, 1999). There is a fear that the values and objectives of academics and other traditional university stakeholders will be diluted or lost if we follow an overly commercial "customer service focus" which emphasises the perceived needs of students to the detriment of these academic values.

Scott is right to state that marketing is not just about giving customers what they want. Customer satisfaction comes from the match between expectation and reality. This is as much about shaping and managing expectations as it is about delivering to them. In order to affect customer and student expectations we need to understand them and assess them: are they appropriate and realistic or justifiable and achievable?

Educational marketing is about building a relationship with the potential students, where we have genuine concern for them rather than merely seeking to fulfill our own needs, like filling a place or making a sale. The educational purchase decision is high risk and complex, requiring significant up-front investment and time commitment, with no immediate or tangible return. Students will only achieve their goal if we as educators deliver but also if they deliver (for example, attend classes or complete assignments). The marketing relationship therefore must be one that is built on trust and authenticity. Bringing into line the expectations of the students/customers and the educators will result in a two-way dialogue, thus building this relationship.

It is not so much that "the customer is always right" but more that "the customer always has rights". This is the customer orientation that universities must develop, coupled with effective ways of assessing and responding to student expectations. It is fair to say that some student expectations are formed by the customer experiences they have elsewhere, for example few are prepared to stand in long queues any more, and few will tolerate inefficient use of time. Of course the advertising and promotion put out by universities will also create expectations.

Student expectations

In order to find a balance, we need to be confident that we can identify and understand the various student expectations. Graham (1998) summarises what customers are looking for. These are transferable to potential students:

- Accurate information that enhances their understanding.

- Options – options create dialogue and interaction which in turn creates relationships. Relationships build the customer base.

- Single source service – services are bundled together and delivered at one point of contact.

- Cutting edge technology – many secondary school students are arriving at university expecting to have access to wireless networks, to transact all their administrative business on line, to have access to latest technology and equipment.

- Communication – universities are expected to be responsive, give timely and full feedback.

- Flexibility and choice – increasingly we see students wanting to chose what they study, how and when, and they do not want to wait around for answers.

- Consulting – just as learning is an interactive discursive process, so is identifying what the student is looking for and establishing the relationship, with mutual respect.

- New ideas – it must be about creativity and innovation. Students have aspirational goals, and they want new ideas that will benefit them.

- Honesty – if we can not meet their needs or their expectations are unrealistic, then we need to say so. The marketing messages must be authentic.

There is a plethora of research available (beyond that which institutions conduct for themselves) looking at why students make the tertiary choices they do and what their perceived expectations are, both what they will experience as tertiary students and what they hope to get out of it.

The financial pressures on students are commonly understood. At Swinburne University of Technology in Victoria, research shows that about 50% of 2001 commencing undergraduate students are in some form of full-time or part-time employment and a further 12% are looking. There are increased demands for flexibility as regards when and how students learn due to the expectations generated from the various technologies. As consumers use the internet to find information, communicate and undertake transactions, they will assume that the education experience can be accessed in the same way.

Increasingly, university studies need to be accommodated around a range of other priorities in students' lives.

Marketing messages to potential students pick up on these needs and feed back promotional images of students studying on-line at the beach over summer; copy which refers to studying in "a time and place that suits you". Even those universities that do not overtly promote flexibility are caught up in the consumers' minds as being able to help them juggle their priorities.

A substantial body of research shows that the single most important expectation potential tertiary students have of a university is that it should improve their chances of getting the sort of job they want. It is often a very vocational or professional and pragmatic decision.

Again, the marketing messages reflect this. Course brochures describe the career opportunities of each course; university testimonials show successfully employed people crediting their alma mater as the stepping-stone to their career. Universities are publicly measured and compared on how successfully they can place graduates in employment.

In a market where we compete for students, we are simply responding to their clearly understood needs.

Mackay (2000) describes the culture of our current senior secondary school students: "they are keeping their options open. Everything is up for grabs ... freedom is a big, big word for them, and uncertainty is its twin". They are a highly educated and over-stimulated generation, and when marketing to them it is "not a matter of talking to them as individuals. You are talking to members of a tribe ... for today's school leavers, personal identity is more group based – less individualistic than ever".

These characteristics will manifest themselves in expectations of university education. The combination of open mindedness and real scepticism for sales and marketing communications means they will be far less tolerant of false or misleading promotional messages. Couple this with the fact that many intending, first time university entrants do not know what to expect and have an untested set of perceptions about what university life will be like. It is highly likely there will be dissatisfaction resulting from the gap between expectations and reality. Universities must take the initiative to deal with this and manage it properly and marketers can contribute significantly to this – if allowed.

What can and should higher education marketers do?

There are six issues which need to be addressed in order to find a meaningful and positive way forward, from the point of view of using the professional marketing expertise already present in universities. The first three are probably quite acceptable and not controversial. The last three are not meant as criticism of current attitudes or approaches, rather they are offered as a way forward.

Watch the pendulum. Marketers need to be constantly aware of what exactly they are promoting and selling and thus all their marketing activity needs to be appropriately designed and executed.

In 1999 Swinburne University of Technology moved away from traditional competitive positioning messages and tried to develop marketing messages that communicated the purpose and intrinsic benefits of learning and study. We tried to find messages that spoke of the aspirational and personal benefits of education and the resulting outcomes, both altruistic and egoistic, thus accommodating the pragmatic expectations already held by potential students, but also communicating the university's broader role in helping create citizens and contributing to society more broadly:

"You will discover your strengths, your voice, your purpose
You will achieve your goals, your ideals, your best
You will change your outlook, your community, your life
You will know your world, your future, yourself."

(Swinburne University of Technology, positioning creative, copyright 1999).

Professional marketers will be very aware that they are creating expectations in the market. The copy, images and channels that we use to communicate, all build pictures of what students will experience and what outcomes they will achieve through study. Universities must let the marketers use their professional judgement and expertise to create appropriate, authentic pictures.

Education about education. It is clear that new entrants to tertiary education do not know what to expect and do not have a good feel for what life will be like within the university. We therefore must do a better job of telling them. There are some great examples of such induction or education communication. Two such examples are: "Race Around Monash", a video for prospective students to Monash University in Melbourne on what to expect as a new undergraduates, and the Tertiary Information Service in Victoria where all Victorian universities and TAFE institutes work collaboratively to educate final year school students on their options and choices.

Use marketers to help discover and define student expectations. Despite the research which has been undertaken to date, we still do not know enough about what students expect. We therefore cannot manage these expectations, or re-orient them to a more realistic or practical level.

Bring down some of the barriers between traditional academic and student administration worlds and the world of marketing and student recruitment. Marketers are sent to find new students for the institution, and then are often asked to manage the on-going relationship with alumni, but are expected to ignore students once they are in the institution. Marketers can develop proper pricing strategies, and should be part of managing and developing the student experience within the institution and should be able to partner with academic and administrative staff.

In the same vein, marketers should probably check that they really do understand and appreciate the products and services they are representing to the market. This is far more than knowing what courses are available, what the entry requirements are and what the career outcomes might be. The learning and teaching process is constantly evolving and developing; marketers need to understand what is happening in the learning model.

Differentiate. Universities need to overcome their fear of being customer or student focussed. We need to be clear about what our mission is and what we are trying to achieve, before we can convince any potential student that we can deliver it for them. By defining what it is that we offer, deliver, develop and contribute, we can then work out where the matches are with market needs and expectations; both pragmatic needs in terms of professional, vocational or economically driven responses and more subtle and fundamental community based, knowledge and societal development responses. We need to find a way to be relevant in the short and long term.

It is not that the customer is always right, but that we need to acknowledge their rights, and be responsive to their needs. We need to keep adapting.

References

CARTWRIGHT, D. and YOUG, C. (1999),
   Assessment of Student Outcomes, Symposium for the Marketing of Higher Education, Truman State University.

GRAHAM, J.R. (1998),
   "What today's customers expect", *American Salesman*, 44(4), pp. 15-23.

KOTLER, P., CHANDLER, P., GIBBS, M. and MCCOLL, R. (1989),
   Marketing Australia, second edition, Prentice Hall.

MACKAY, H. (2000),
   Leaving School, Mackay Report.

PRAHALAD, C. and HAMEL, G. (1994),
   Competing for the Future, Harvard Business School Press.

ROTTMEYER, L. and LINAMEN, L. (1999),
   "Just around the corner, a marketing oriented look at the future of higher education", Dallas Baptist University.

SANDER, P., STEVENSON, K., KING, M. and COATES, D. (2000),
   "University Students' Expectations of Teaching", *Studies in Higher Education*, 25(3), pp. 309-324.

SCOTT, S.V. (1999),
   "The academic as service provider: is the customer always right?", *Journal of Higher Education Policy and Management*, 21(2), pp. 193-203.

WALSHE, R. (2001),
   Unitec, Brand Performance and a Customer Voice, Marketing Education Conference.

A Survey of Student-institution Relationships in Europe

Dennis Farrington

Most research on students is about how they should become more closely involved in issues that affect education itself, in evaluation, the renovation of teaching methods and curricula and, in the institutional framework in force, in policy formulation and institutional management. There has until now been no attempt to provide a synthesis of the legal and constitutional position of students within Europe.

Such a synthesis is important for six reasons. First, to understand why countries make different provision for regulating the relationship between service provider and recipient in what is essentially the same service. Second, although the position of "international" students is often regulated rather differently from that of domiciled students, "mobile" students have no comprehensive guide to their position. Third, as increasing globalisation of higher education takes place, those taking part should know their legal position in the event of a dispute or claim. Fourth, the World Student Congress is focusing on student rights. Fifth, the Budapest *Declaration for a Greater Europe Without Dividing Lines* underlines the role of universities as sites of citizenship, implying new roles and obligations for students. Sixth, building on the Council of Europe's Legislative Reform Programme, individual governments might wish to consider some form of harmonisation of this and other aspects of higher education regulation through framework laws.

This chapter is an overview of a full report which identifies a range of provisions in constitutions, education and higher education laws and internal regulations dealing with student rights and obligations and how they are enforced (Farrington, 2000). It proposes that certain fundamental rights and obligations should be common across Europe, linking this with the implementation of the Lisbon Convention, the Sorbonne and Bologna Declarations.

The legal relationship

The student relationship with the publicly-funded universities in Europe is not easy to define. The Anglo-American trend towards applying at least in part a contractual analogy with private providers is not recognised in all European countries, to some extent due to the differences between the Humboldtian, Anglo-Saxon and Napoleonic models of higher education. In some states, public universities do not enjoy full legal personality. At least in part, the provision of education funded by the public purse is often seen as a form of social contract between State and student. This is not just reflected in the "state orders for specialists" which formed an integral part of the Soviet Union higher education system and remains in common parlance in some countries today, but also in the concept reflected in statements such as:

- "The purpose of university education is to prepare people to become high-level managers and professionals capable of taking responsibility in fundamental and applied research and in the planning and application of scientific research with a view to the development of new technologies" (Kaufmann, 1996, p. 115).

- "The main purpose of higher education is to ensure the training of highly qualified specialists in all spheres of activity" (Gaugaç, 1996, p. 217).

- "The goal/mission of the higher civil education is ... to train high cadres ... [and] to prepare new scientists".[5]

- "The aim of higher education shall be to train highly qualified experts above and beyond secondary education".[6]

Whatever the expressed aims or goals, it is perhaps a reasonable expectation of the taxpayer that students will take full and proper advantage of the publicly-funded opportunities open to them, which shifts thinking to some extent towards a concentration on the obligations, rather than on the rights, of students. Competitive access to higher education provided by the State is a constitutional right in some countries and the laws of these and other countries contain guarantees which would not be recognised as appropriate in the United Kingdom.

My view is that "...the status of students has changed irrevocably. The change has been from one of being in a subordinate role in the *studium generale* to one of a consumer of services" (Farrington, 1998, p. 307). When in 1967 the American Association of University Professors (AAUP) and four other organisations[7] drafted the joint statement on Rights and Freedoms of Students this was seen as articulating a set of principles that seemed revolutionary to educators. At the time, many expected higher education to "continue its previous course in which students were merely passive recipients of education" (Mullendore, 1992). In establishing these principles, AAUP was already aware that the courts were beginning to accept the existence of a contract between student and institution, at least in private universities, later extended to public institutions (Kaplin and Lee, 1995, pp. 373-377). Now, in the common law university world, it is increasingly accepted that the basic underlying rights of student and institution are contractual, the free formation of a contract being modified to some extent by statute law and regulation, either governmental or internal.

As an illustration, in the United Kingdom it is trite law that a potential student may be denied a place without the institution having to give any reason, which distinguishes higher education from most other types of "public service" largely funded by the taxpayer. No contract is ever formed so that the student is in a sense being treated as if he or she were a customer in a shop, making an invitation to treat prior to the conclusion of a bargain. In other countries, access to publicly-funded higher education is an absolute right (except in a limited number of expensive disciplines) if basic conditions for admission are met. So there is no argument that, if the contractual analogy were to hold in these countries, the institution would be forced to enter into a contract. That in itself would raise interesting questions about the extent of a university's legal obligations towards a student whom it has not selected for academic ability. The introduction of high tuition fees in some countries makes consumers of students and their families, in line with principles of privatisation and individual responsibility: the "user-pays" philosophy (UNESCO, 1998). Universities enter into competition with each other and vie with each other to offer high quality services in return for demanding high fees. Cogent arguments against this competitive situation are that it both undermines co-operation between institutions and stifles free exchange of ideas. In fact, we have seen much more emphasis in recent years on the protection of institutional intellectual property rights, particularly in markets where private providers are encroaching, for example in Web-based educational courses.

If the contract analogy is not accepted, then as citizens in receipt of public services students may proceed to challenge the activities of universities by a public law process, akin to judicial review in the United Kingdom. Indeed, it is clear that in a number of countries the concept of a contract between students and institutions does not exist in the Anglo-American sense and that everything is founded on public law.

Access

In the language of international conventions, "no person shall be denied the right to education"[8] and "higher education shall be accessible to all on the basis of merit".[9] Access to higher education, *i.e.* general eligibility for higher education programmes, is distinguished from admission, *i.e.* gaining a study place, which may be on a selective basis. Access should in principle be open to all; denial of the right of access on a competitive basis to start educational institutions existing as a given time may be in breach of the first sentence of Article 2 of the *First Protocol to the Convention for the Protection of Human Rights and Fundamental Freedoms* (ECHR): "no person shall be denied the right to education". Where certain limited higher

117

education facilities are provided by a State, in principle it is not incompatible with Article 2 of Protocol No. 1 to restrict access thereto to those students who have attained the academic level required to most benefit from the courses offered. It is a typical provision in the new constitutions of the 1990s, freed from communism, to guarantee the right to education in a positive way and in some instances build in guarantees of free tuition, for example in Belarus, Lithuania and Bulgaria. In other ex-communist states, such as Slovakia, a similar provision is made in law. Some countries without a communist past, including Finland and Belgium, also provide for higher education in their constitutional law.

Some modern framework laws translate the right of access in a non-discriminatory way, at least in respect of the citizens of the State concerned. For example, the *Law on Education of Romania* (1995) provides in Article 5(1) for equal rights of access to all levels and forms of education to Romanian citizens "irrespective of their social or material background, sex, race, nationality, political or religious belonging". Another example is the right set out in the Spanish *Right to Education (Organic) Act* 1985 to go on to higher education levels without any distinction on grounds of a student's financial situation, social class or place of residence. Article 3 of the *Education Act* 1998 of the Republic of Malta makes similar provision and Article 41(1) provides: "In ... the University all teaching shall be given to Maltese Citizens without any fee being charged".

The general tradition in new member states of the Council of Europe (the countries of the former Soviet Union and other central and Eastern European states) was to select students for entry to higher education on the basis of a form of manpower planning called "state orders for specialists" which itself led to a highly regulated, restrictive curriculum, the consequences of which are still with us in some member states of the former Soviet Union.

Selection corresponds to a cleavage within Western Europe. In some countries, there is either no selection at all from those who have passed the relevant school-leaving examination or partial selection for specific disciplines, notably medicine. In others, on the one hand there is the *numerus clausus* system and on the other the system in which selection is at the discretion of the higher education institution concerned, sometimes by examination. Selection may also apply only to some programmes, and different criteria may be applied to different programmes, particularly those leading automatically or partially to a professional licence to practice, *e.g.* in teaching, medicine or law or to particular types of institution such as the *Grandes Écoles* in France. Selection criteria and number of places available may vary over time as subjects wax and wane in popularity, economic prospects for employment grow or diminish ("state orders for specialists" having largely disappeared from the scene as the market economy replaces state monopoly), public demand for professionals increases or decreases. The principle of selective entry cannot therefore be challenged as contrary to some European "norm" – in fact, as more member states were admitted selection became the "norm" – but whatever the system it has to be fair.

Many countries do not have a centralised admissions service for entry at basic level so that each institution has responsibility for its own admissions. This inevitably raises questions of transparency and fairness of the admissions process to all applicants. As the Council of Europe acknowledges, this is a complex problem involving matters such as the scheme of school-leaving assessment, entrance examinations and independent tests, clearing houses, statistical monitoring, and European practice is very diverse (Council of Europe, 2000, p. 40, Part II, para. 5.1.1.).

Admission qualifications vary and in order to be able to take full advantage of the provisions of the 1997 Recognition Convention[10] potential entrants need to have some idea not only what they are (a process facilitated by the network arrangements set up under the Convention and its predecessors and by the European Union) but how they are applied fairly in practice. Article III.1(2) prohibits discrimination on any of the grounds set out in ECHR or on the grounds of any other circumstance not related to the merits of the qualification or period of study for which recognition is sought. This requires the parties to the 1997 Convention to make appropriate arrangements for the assessment of an application for recognition of qualifications and periods of study solely on the basis of the knowledge and skills achieved and to ensure by appropriate means that higher education institutions co-operate in this process. To this end a number of countries provide detailed guidance on their higher education systems to intending foreign applicants. Some countries have entered reservations on acceding to the recognition Convention or its predecessors, for example Germany in respect of access to the professions, or made a declaration in relation to cases in which normal procedure for validation of foreign qualifications and other matters is not followed, for example France in relation to medicine, pharmacy and dental surgery. Some countries, such as Belgium, insist on reciprocity.

The Confederation of European Union Rectors' Conferences and the Association of European Universities (CRE) in their project report on trends in learning structures in higher education suggest four main avenues of combined action which may foster the desired convergence and transparency in qualification structures in Europe. These are:

- The gradual adoption of an ECTS-compatible credit accumulation system.
- The adoption of a common, but flexible frame of reference for qualifications.
- An enhanced European dimension in quality assurance, evaluation and accreditation.
- Empowering Europeans to use the new learning opportunities (CEURC/CRE, 1999).

119

For the purposes of this report, the emphasis on structural improvements is important, since they would help to eliminate obstacles to student mobility. The combined impact of the suggested actions would make European higher education more understandable and attractive to students from other continents. I would add to the conclusions of the Confederation and Association that a common framework of basic student rights and obligations would assist the processes of understanding and mobility.

The 1997 convention includes the concept of an applicant's right to receive a reply to a request for recognition of qualifications or periods of study within a reasonable time. It does not prescribe a deadline, unlike the European Union General Directives on professional recognition, which prescribe a deadline of four months. In the event of an unsuccessful application, the authority evaluating it has to show why it does not fulfil the requirements for recognition. This relates to the applicant's right to appeal, arrangements and procedures for such appeals being subject to the legislation in force in the country concerned. The handling of such appeals should be subject to the same requirements of transparency, coherence and reliability as those imposed on the original assessment of the application. An example of such a procedure is that adopted by Lithuania in 2000. In order to formulate an appeal, it is argued that an appellant needs some information by way of precedent on what they can realistically expect. On the other hand, there is a danger of establishing too rigid legal precedents for the "automatic" processing of applications. This issue has attracted the attention of the ENIC/NARIC Working Group on Criteria and Procedures for the assessment of foreign qualifications, resolved in favour of giving applicants information on typical outcomes, with a clear understanding that in all cases an individual assessment of the application is undertaken.

Financial support for students

Sophisticated systems for financial support have not been confined to Western Europe. Indeed in the period before the 1990s many central and eastern European countries prided themselves on free (that is, non-paying) access and provision of state stipends to higher education students. This was not confined to the Soviet Union and its satellites: until 1987, Malta had a Worker-Student scheme under which students received salaries from their employers. Now, there is tension between free access, as explained above a constitutional right in some countries, and budgetary provision, generally inadequate to sustain the old support system at the same level in real cash terms. A typical solution has been to take one step further the idea of "fees-only" student places in addition to those subsidised by the State but at the same level of tuition fee (the UK system).

The result is a two-tier system in which students compete for an arguably inadequate number of state-subsidised free places and, failing to secure one of those, can then compete for entry at market-level fees to an additional quota of places which the institution is licensed to offer. Apart from fundamental questions about the licensing arrangements and the criteria (physical norms, standards of staff, adequacy of support services), this practice raises questions of differential quotas in popular subjects, virement of places between subjects and fairness. The procedure has been criticised as unfair and inefficient by the Council of Europe and the OECD. In doing so, two principles have been formulated: that equal access requires financial support differentiated according to need; and that any fees should be partial, reasonable in level, and uniform across the public system. These norms are explicit in Council of Europe Recommendation R(98)3. However, these principles remain controversial. The first is superficially similar to the discredited class-based admission preferences of the past. The second requires "abandoning a convenient myth" (Council of Europe, 2000, p. 40, Part II, para. 5.1.2.).

A study on the topic of student support was published by EURYDICE (the European Commission's information network on education in Europe) in 1999 (EURYDICE, 1999, p. 186). This study is restricted to the Member States of the European Union. The comparative analysis revealed wide variations between countries in the components of support systems: grants, loans, etc; targeting of students for support; etc. In all countries, the State assumes a greater responsibility for funding undergraduate education in public universities than does the student or the student's family. In some countries (Iceland, Liechtenstein, Luxembourg) a large proportion of students studies abroad. The United Kingdom introduced general tuition fees in 1998 (a position partially reversed in Scotland in 2000) whereas Ireland abolished them. Some countries with no tuition fees (for example Germany, Greece and Austria) place emphasis on the responsibility of the family, as do others which do charge tuition fees (France, Ireland, Belgium, Spain, Portugal and Italy). The details of these systems are beyond the scope of this report. Others, notably the Scandinavian countries, emphasise the financial independence of students vis-à-vis their parents. However, the latter also have a policy of no tuition fees.

Where the emphasis is placed on the student paying his/her own way through loans, a path along which the United Kingdom has moved steadily over the past decade, and particularly where tuition fees are also payable, we might expect a correlation with the view of students as customers or consumers of higher education paying for educational services.

In some new member states there are provisions for students who perform exceptionally to switch from fee-paying to free at the end of any particular year. Such processes have to be managed fairly and openly. In the European Union, the award of support appears more closely related to study achievement where it is allocated on a substantial scale in so far as it is available to a large proportion of students and includes large amounts in the form of grants. In such cases, to quote EURYDICE, students typically not only have the obligation to do well but "to do well quickly" since support is time-limited (EURYDICE, 1999, Profile No. 44, pp. 19, 22).

Rights and obligations of students

A discussion of the specific rights and obligations of students has to take place against a background of who students are and what they might expect from universities in meeting their learning needs. Students, it can be said, "... participate voluntarily, in a study or professional training programme, a choice which they make more consciously and independently than their orientation during secondary education" (Fiers and Lesseliers, 1996, p. 109). Establishing what the needs of these voluntary participants are can be bedevilled by ambiguities, complexities and ideological differences. Nevertheless one outcome of a Workshop on Lifelong Learning for Equality and Social Cohesion (Council of Europe, 1999, p. 6) was that students might reasonably expect the following practical and achievable things from universities:

- Flexible, shorter courses taught at a time and place convenient to students.

- Competent teachers who can communicate complex ideas in a clear and accessible way.

- Teachers and programmes which respect, utilise and give credit for learning which takes place in a wide range or settings outside higher education.

- Honesty about what is on offer and about the labour market implications of study (noting that increasing educational opportunities does not always increase employment opportunities).

- Higher education institutions which know who their students are, which find out and respect the motivations of their students, whether these be job-related or personal development.

Some of these aspirations can be reflected in law or regulation depending on the extent of state control of public universities:

- Creating flexibility within the national framework of qualifications – as adjusted to fit with the Bologna model and international credit-transfer systems.

- Licensing, accreditation and quality audit processes which encourage institutions, whether through financial inducements/penalties or otherwise to put in place a sound internal quality assurance system.

- Penalising deliberately or negligently misleading advertising and other inducements to study.

- Putting in place workable training, development and appraisal systems for staff and enhancing professional status and pride in work through proper remuneration and conditions of service, initiatives such as the Institute for Learning and Teaching in Higher Education in the United Kingdom.

From a more legalistic viewpoint, as part of the contract with the university the student might expect:

- A statement of the course or programme which the institution has agreed to provide and the resources available to support it including a safe working environment supportive of study.

- A clear statement of the academic and financial obligations of the student in respect of that course of programme.

- A list of the circumstances under which the course, the programme and (if relevant) its location may be varied by the institution or under which the student may apply to vary the course or programme.

- A clear statement of the disciplinary rules applicable to the student both in relation to academic and non-academic activities.

- A clear statement of arrangements, if any, for appeals against failure to meet specified academic or non-academic obligations or penalties imposed for breach of discipline.

- A comprehensive, accessible, fair complaints procedure (Farrington, 1998, para. 4.140).

There are of course other ways of classifying these rights, including "legal competencies in a democratically governed higher education system" and "a general right to be consulted by the competent authorities when matters concern student affairs in the broadest sense of the word, including academic and social affairs and general management" (Council of Europe, 1995).

At the very least students should be assured that they will be treated fairly. Introduction of procedures such as double-marking, second supervisors, anonymous examination scripts, external examining, neutral and independent appeal procedures and appropriate sanctions goes some way towards meeting this objective.

We might add a right, as reflected for example in Section 14 of the German Federal Framework Law for Higher Education, to suitable academic counselling. As the Confederation of European Rectors' Conferences/CRE have pointed out, a survey of the first years of tertiary education carried out by OECD (OECD, 1998), as well as an impressive number of national inquiries and reports, have shown the essential role of information and counselling, and the severe consequences that happen when students enter study courses which they have not chosen, or are confronted with requirements they did not expect or cannot meet. The Confederation/ CRE report states:

"A European space for higher education would require additional efforts at European, national and institutional level to raise the level of information to students and ensure a better fit between expectations of institutions of higher education and their students" (CEURC/CRE, 1999, section III).

Some of these rights coincide with those set out over 30 years ago in the US *Joint Statement on Rights and Freedoms of Students* mentioned earlier (Mullendore, 1992, 13-22). Although much of that statement was concerned with protection of rights established in the US Constitution, echoed to a considerable degree by those set out in the ECHR (freedom of expression and association, protection of privacy) they also included protection against improper academic evaluation and the establishment of procedural standards in disciplinary proceedings. In the context of the time, it is not surprising that issues concerned with discipline took up a large amount of space.

Students' obligations include:

- To study to the best of their abilities, take examinations and try to finish their studies.
- To behave as responsible persons respecting legitimate regulations, inside and outside the institutions.
- To pay tuition fees if any, and pay back study loans according to the regulations (Council of Europe, 1995).

As a concrete example of this, in Italy, the principal obligations are:

- To pay fees.
- To attend class when required.
- To give respectful consideration to university dignity and honour.
- Not to damage university buildings or any other kind of its immovable and movable property.
- Not to prevent the regular development of university courses and academic activities (IMUSTR, 2000, p. 21).

Specific obligations may be imposed: for example in Cyprus where students must receive an overall average of seven for each semester of study, or be placed on probation, with a view to termination if the average remains below seven. In addition, limits may be placed on university powers to reflect basic rights, for example in Italy a student may not be excluded "temporarily" from a university for more than three years. This is in the context of legal provisions for dealing with disorder dating to 1935 and still in force.

Some norms are unusual reflecting the less developed democratic state of some countries. For example, in Belarus the operative law is directed principally at satisfying the needs of the economy so contains requirements on students to work after graduation and recently a suggestion was made for a contract between the student and the state for the provision of financial support in return for work. There is a similar arrangement in Ukraine: Article 52(2) of its 1996 Law provides:

"Graduates of higher educational establishments who received education at the expenses of state or local budgets can be sent to work and are obliged to work at the assigned job in a manner determined by the Cabinet of Ministers of Ukraine."

The rights and obligations of a student may be established at different levels in different states according to the normative hierarchy generally adopted by the Council of Europe, *i.e.* in primary legislation (or sometimes, in relation to free access or other basic rights, in the Constitution itself), in secondary legislation (government orders, decrees, etc.) and/or in the charters, statutes or other governing instruments of the institutions.

An example of a constitutional law which provides basic rights in addition to the right of access is the German Basic law (*Grundgetsetz*) which in Article 5(3) provides for freedom of study. This is defined in Section 4(4) of the Federal Framework Law:

"Freedom of study shall – notwithstanding the study and examination regulations – include, in particular, the free choice of classes, the right to establish one's own priorities within a course of study an the formulation and expression by students of their own opinions on artistic and scientific subject-matter. Decisions on study may be taken by the competent university bodies to the extent that they relate to the organisation and proper implementation of teaching and studying activities and to guaranteeing the orderly pursuit of studies."

Laws may simply set out a framework within which other forms of legislation and university constitutions operate. The revisions to the German Federal Framework Law by the Fourth amendment Law of 1998 provide an example of deregulation. The amendments removed detailed provisions for, *inter alia*, examination regulations, study regulations, subjects and classes to be offered, "student order" (provisions governing the cancellation of registration of students who obstructed the normal operation of a university), composition of bodies, voting rights, elections and administration. The law retains in addition to freedom of study defined above, some quite detailed requirements in Section 14 for academic counselling:

"The institution of higher education shall inform students and applicants on the opportunities and conditions of study and on the content, structure and requirements of study courses. During the entire period of study it shall assist students by providing subject-oriented advice. At the end of the first year of study, it shall determine the students' progress, inform the students and, if necessary, provide guidance and counselling. In providing such guidance, the

125

institution shall co-operate in particular with both the authorities responsible for vocationial guidance and those responsible for state examinations."

Student rights and obligations may also be derived from any contractual relationship recognised to exist between an individual and the institution, at any stage in the overall process from application to graduation. Where legislation defines some aspects of the relationship, it may not just be specific education or higher education legislation but other kinds of legislation, for example on health and safety. In the United Kingdom and Ireland there may be some elements derived from common law, for example the law of contract where unregulated by statute, or the law of negligence. In countries with a Civil Code there may be relevant sections impinging on the relationship. There may be interaction between public and private law where such distinctions exist and are broadly comparable.

Although proposals have been made for a student charter having some supra-national effect (UNESCO, 1998) this could only be a statement of principles. More likely is the accompanying proposal for a charter by 2005 promoting and protecting the rights of international students within perhaps the framework established by the recognition Convention discussed earlier.

In some countries student rights may be clearly set out in rulebooks *e.g.* section 5 of the Austrian *Allgemeines Hochschul-Studentgesetz* or they may be set out in the Charter or equivalent of the university as in Romania. In the United Kingdom, apart from provisions about tuition fees and loans, there is no legislation on student rights, all of which must be discerned from individual university constitutions and publications.

There is clearly a wide disparity between the different European countries in the extent to which student rights and obligations are established in primary education legislation. These range from highly detailed provisions (*e.g.* Bulgaria) through more general statements of fundamental rights (*e.g.* Germany) through to nothing at all, apart from the obligation to pay fees and rights to loans (United Kingdom).

Appendix 3 to the report (Farrington, 2000) suggests an allocation to the various levels of legislation of topics culled from an earlier investigation and report into governance. On the assumption that fundamental rights and duties of students *qua* citizens generally are established in the constitutional (and, often, administrative) law of the country concerned, be it in the form of a written constitution or common law, and that some specific rights *e.g.* the right to education, are similarly established, the report suggested that primary education legislation need only:

- Delimit the powers of public institutions to charge fees to local and non-local students.

- Describe in general terms systems for student financial support.

- Describe in general terms rights of students and staff to organise.

Secondary legislation, where this is a feature of the legal system, should:

- Prescribe details of student support arrangements.
- Prescribe arrangements for public institutions charging fees to different groups of students.

The different legal systems combine these in different ways, so it is probably best to treat these two as a combined level: issues for the state and Parliament or Ministers. The mechanisms for setting of fees and for securing the right to higher education through adequate student support dominates this list.

Internal rules, which are a feature of all systems examined, should:

- Delimit membership of institution (including students).
- Regulate admission of students, progress and discipline.
- Provide for student organisations.
- Regulate arrangements for student accommodation, etc.
- Regulate mechanism for making academic awards.

The reason for leaving most of the details to the institution is to uphold as far as possible the autonomy of the institution and to enable some flexibility of approach in delivering a quality educational service to an increasingly discerning group of "clients".

Enforcement of rights: complaints and appeals

Most commentators and analysts would agree that litigation between students and universities is something to be avoided. Litigation is a slow and bumpy ride, particularly as the litigant normally has to pay. "Ambulance chasing" takes on a new meaning. Easing the less successful student's path and trying to keep the student away from that ambulance lies at the heart of reforms in complaints and appeals procedures in many countries over the past decade.

There is a close relationship between a discussion of student complaints and quality assurance. A mechanism for resolution of issues arising in the academic sphere, with objectively verifiable reasons given for failure to resolve them in the student's favour, is an essential part of a university's quality control process. Likewise feedback from complaints and appeals, successful or not, is an essential input into review and monitoring of courses and academic procedures.

The extent to which a student may complain to a non-judicial body such as a Ministry reflects the differences in the autonomy of universities in different systems. The introduction of Ombudsmen or similar provisions is a measure designed to keep student disputes out of the ordinary courts. There are many

127|

examples detailed in the published report of such provisions at national level, the United Kingdom notably lagging behind.

Appendix 3 to the full report (Farrington, 2000) also suggests that at State level there should be established minimum requirements for the effective resolution of internal disputes. A number of countries have recognised that wherever possible student disputes should be kept out of court. First there should be an attempt to resolve them internally using for example the Latvian example of an internal court of arbitration. Once the issue is externalised, mechanisms such as Malta's Ombudsman can come into play.

However, Appendix 3 also suggests that providing mechanisms for resolving disputes between students and the institution should be left to the internal rules of the institution. Again this is to preserve the autonomy of the institution in making decisions about its members.

Further action

The report suggests that Member States of the Council of Europe may wish to re-examine, in the context of the developments set out at the start of the report, whether they have:

- Allocated competency for determining student rights and obligations to an appropriate level in their education law.
- Described student rights and obligations clearly, in a way which can be understood by any European student.
- Provided appropriate modern mechanisms for handling student complaints and appeals.

Notes

5. Article 2, Law on Higher Education, Law No. 8461 Albania (1999).

6. Article 2, *Higher Education Act*, Bulgaria (1995).

7. The Association of American Colleges, the United States National Student Association, The National Association of Student Personnel Administrators and the National Association for Women Deans and Counsellors.

8. Article 2 of the First Protocol to the Convention for the Protection of Human Rights and Fundamental Freedoms (ECHR): (ETS No.5, 1950), Protocol adopted in Paris, 20 March 1952.

9. Universal Declaration of Human Rights (1948), Article 26; International Covenant on Economic, Social and Cultural Rights (1965,) Article 13(2); Council of Europe Recommendation R (98)3 on access to higher education; and as to access by minorities, Framework Convention for the Protection of National Minorities (ETS No. 157, 1995).

10. Convention on the Recognition of Qualifications concerning Higher Education in the European Region (ETS No. 135, 1997), The United Kingdom has signed but not ratified the Convention.

References

CONFEDERATION OF EUROPEAN RECTORS' CONFERENCES/CRE (1999),
   Trends in Learning Structures in Higher Education.

COUNCIL OF EUROPE (1995),
   DECS LRP 95/16, *The position of students.*

COUNCIL OF EUROPE (1999),
   DECS/EDU/HE (99) 44.

COUNCIL OF EUROPE (2000),
   CC-HER.

EURYDICE (1999),
   Key Topics in Education, Vol. 1, Financial Support for Students in Higher Education in Europe, Trends and Debates.

FARRINGTON, D.J. (1998),
   The Law of Higher Education, Butterworths, London.

FARRINGTON, D.J. (2000),
   "A study of student-institution relationships in selected member states of the Council of Europe", *European Journal for Education Law and Policy* 4(2), pp. 99-120.

FIERS, J. and LESSELIERS, J. (1996),
   "The Flemish Community of Belgium", in R. In't Veld, H-P Füssel and G. Neave, *Relations between State and Higher Education*, Kluwer Law International.

GAUGAÇ, P. (1996),
   "Moldova", in R. In't Veld, H-P Füssel and G. Neave, *op. cit.*

ITALIAN MINISTRY FOR UNIVERSITIES AND SCIENTIFIC AND TECHNOLOGICAL RESEARCH (2000),
   Higher Education in Italy – A Guide for Foreigners (CIMEA of the RUI Foundation).

KAPLIN, W.A. and LEE, B.A. (1995),
   The Law of Higher Education, 3rd ed., Jossey-Bass, San Francisco.

KAUFMANN, C. (1996),
   "The French Community of Belgium", in R. In't Veld, H-P Füssel and G. Neave, *op. cit.*

MULLENDORE, R.H. (1992),
   "The 'Joint Statement on Rights and Freedoms of Students': Twenty-Five Years Later", in W.A. Bryan, R.H. Mullendore (eds), *Rights Freedoms and Responsibilities of Students*, Jossey-Bass, San Francisco.

OECD (1998),
   Redefining Tertiary Education.

UNESCO (1998),
   Thematic Debate Higher Education for a New Society: A Student Vision section III: *www.unesco.org/ education/educprog/wche/principal/student.html*

Responding to Legal Liability

Anthony P. Moore

The principle of liability

The application of legal liability to educators was emphatically endorsed by the British House of Lords in 2000. The fundamental principle was stated by Lord Nicholls as follows:

"If a teacher carelessly teaches the wrong syllabus for an external examination and provable financial loss follows, why should there be no liability" (Phelps v. Hillingdon London Borough Council, 2000, 3 WLR 776 at 804).

The case involved four separate claims against local school authorities by students with disabilities. Three of the cases involved students with dyslexia and one a sufferer from Duchenne muscular dystrophy. In all cases the schools had failed to recognise or respond to the special needs of these children.

In all cases the children and their families were able to show significant financial loss through the cost of alternative arrangements or missed opportunities. One of the children was, for example, awarded GBP 45 650 on the basis that she had had to leave school early and pay for private tuition.

The decision was based on an assessment of the potential liability of educators and placed them on the same footing as the range of professionals such as architects, doctors and financial advisors. Significantly the decision was made in the context of a public education system where the local authorities are under a statutory duty to provide education to residents within their area. They could be described as performing a social rather than a commercial function.

The liability of Australian tertiary education providers towards their students seems equally clear. The arguments for legal liability are in fact probably stronger as all tertiary students are incurring financial obligations for their course even if that obligation is being met by some form of scholarship. There has also been a considerable effort to market tertiary courses as a product and to emphasise competition between tertiary bodies in the provision of courses.

For almost all Australian tertiary courses fees are imposed either directly or by means of liability under a debt repaid to the Federal Government on an income-contingent basis through the taxation system (the Higher Education Contribution Scheme or HECS). The fact of a student obligation being by way of HECS liability will not deprive the arrangement between the educational institution and the student of the character of a contract (in any event the student pays some immediate charges). The fact that the course is being provided under a HECS scheme should not take it out of the commercial context though again the educational institution is not a free agent with respect to the quality of the education provided. Government policy dictates the funds available for any course and any law school administrator knows that law students pay the highest level of HECS charges and under the relative funding model receive the lowest level of funding.

The liability of the English local authorities was based on the general legal doctrine of negligence and Australian tertiary institutions could be sued on this basis. A stronger basis of liability would seem to be the fair trading provisions of the national *Trade Practices Act* 1974 and the equivalent State Fair Trading Acts. In many cases a fair trading claim would be likely to be joined with a negligence claim.

The fair trading context

The fair trading context of legal responsibility for fee-paying tertiary courses has two key concepts: those of avoiding deceptive or misleading statements and of performing tasks with reasonable care and skill. These concepts arise against a characterisation of a trading corporation providing educational services to fee-paying clients. This characterisation places educational services alongside most products in the market-place and applies the traditional requirements of truth in advertising and merchantable quality of products.

What can be startling is the apparent open-endedness of potential liability. For educators a good illustration is that of writing a reference for a student. If the reference is too kind the writer faces a potential action by an employer who has taken on someone regarded as a dud – the employer is suing for lost hiring and training expenses. On the other hand if the reference is too harsh the writer faces potential action by the student who has missed out on a job and is suing for lost income.

The issue of legal liability arises in a culture of greater resort to litigation. The dissatisfied student wants a remedy. A legal system provides remedies that are commercial in nature – commonly compensation for losses. The more education is viewed as training services provided to clients the easier it is for these remedies to seem appropriate. Fee-paying tertiary courses are more likely to have a vocational direction and to reinforce the commercial connotations.

The starting points in terms of fair trading liability in Australia are section 52 of the *Trade Practices Act* 1974 and section 74 of that Act. Section 52 imposes liability for misleading or deceptive conduct. It provides:

- A corporation shall not, in trade or commerce, engage in conduct that is misleading or deceptive or is likely to mislead or deceive.

- Nothing in the succeeding provisions of this Division shall be taken as limiting by implication the generality of sub-section 1).

Section 74 imposes liability to exercise reasonable care and skill in the provision of services. It provides:

- In every contract for the supply by a corporation in the course of a business of services to a consumer there is an implied warranty that the services will be rendered with due care and skill and that any materials supplied in connection with those services will be reasonably fit for the purpose for which they are supplied.

- Where a corporation supplies services (other than services of a professional nature provided by a qualified architect or engineer) to a consumer in the course of a business and the consumer, expressly or by implication, makes known to the corporation any particular purpose for which the services are required or the result that he desires the services to achieve, there is an implied warranty that the services supplied under the contract for the supply of the services and any materials supplied in connection with those services will be reasonably fit for that purpose or are of such a nature and quality that they might reasonably be expected to achieve that result, except where the circumstances show that the consumer does not rely, or that it is unreasonable for him to rely, on the corporation's skill or judgement.

There are some technical issues that arise in the application of these sections to institutions providing fee-paying services. The reference to a corporation in the sections is as a result of the definition section a reference to a trading or financial institution. Furthermore section 52 is confined to statements made in trade or commerce and section 74 confined to services provided in the course of business. It is now likely that a University will be regarded as a trading corporation and the supply of education an act in trade or commerce and in the course of business.* There would be greater room for doubt in the case of educational services provided by a State government education authority both as to the trading corporation characterisation and the possible protection of the shield of State instrumentality immunity from the Commonwealth legislation. Those technical

---

* See Quickendan v O'Connor (1999), FCA 1257 (in the context of the Workplace Relations Act (1996) and Fennell v. Australian National University (1999), FCA 989.

issues relate to policy considerations in that an objection to the quality of education may be an attack on staffing levels which may be set as a matter of State government policy.

Three other points should be made about the scope of liability:

- Section 52 applies to statements about the future (because of section 51a) and with respect to future statements a corporation must establish that it had reasonable grounds for any prediction.

- Vicarious liability applies for the acts of any employee or agent (section 84) so that an institution cannot avoid liability for the acts of any one in that institution and as well any individual knowingly involved in a contravention is personally liable (section 79).

- Liability under section 52 cannot be disclaimed and liability under section 74 cannot be varied or excluded in any contract but a statement can be worded so that it is not an absolute undertaking and thus overall not misleading.

As well as the provisions of the *Trade Practices Act* there are parallel provisions (at least for section 52) in the Fair Trading Acts of the States and Territories. These provisions may avoid some of the technical issues such as whether a trading corporation is involved. In New Zealand there is an equivalent provision in section 9 of the *Fair Trading Act* 1986. The implied obligation to provide services with reasonable care and skill is now very likely to represent the common law obligation and the statutory framework merely removes the possible efficacy of exclusion clauses for which some means of avoidance is likely to be found in any event.

Students seeking redress

In stressing the potential legal liability a writer can appear to overstate the risks involved for educational institutions. Some balance can be gained by pointing out that there has hardly been a flood of cases where educational institutions have been sued. Indeed there has not been a flood of cases brought by consumers with respect to statements made to them or the quality of goods or services supplied to them. It remains the case that the *Trade Practices Act* has overwhelmingly allowed for actions by rival traders against one another and the consumer benefit has been that these actions have stamped out misleading practices.

The reason for the absence of consumer actions is generally said to be the problem of litigation costs. Even if a consumer wanting to sue can find a lawyer prepared to act on a "no win, no fee" basis there remains the threat of liability for the opposing side's costs if unsuccessful. So the significance of the fair trading requirement is more likely to be for negotiated claims and small claims actions. In the educational context the problems of litigation costs are reinforced by problems

134

of establishing losses. In our reference example, I assumed that the poor refer-ence led to the loss of a job. But how could that consequence be established? Similarly if a student is wanting more than a refund for a substandard course how can the student establish any loss in terms of consequential action? Similarly statements in course brochures may be inaccurate but consequences are hard to contemplate unless a promise is made of fulfilling some professional or trade standard that is not fulfilled.

As well as the difficulty of pointing to actual loss a student must establish a failure of proper performance. Lord Nicholls emphasised this need as a reason why the decision in favour of liability would not open the floodgates of legal actions. The door would not be opened for claims based on poor-quality teaching; students would have to prove incompetence or negligence leading to specific mistakes.

In Australia disquiet seems to have been greatest in two main areas: students taking distance education courses and overseas students. But even for these stu-dents the main arguments have been on matters which are difficult to quantify, such as access to lecturers. As a long-serving legal educator the context might have change but the substance of the complaint has not.

There are a couple of procedural points which may assist a student seeking to make a claim. Since the claim may well be based on a breach of the *Trade Practices Act* or a State or Territory Fair Trading Act, the student could approach the Australian Competition and Consumer Commission or the State or Territory Office of Fair Trading or Consumer Affairs. An error in a brochure or other promotional material carries potential criminal liability and the authorities are likely at least to investi-gate a claim of such a breach. But even in respect of a claim of a lack of due care the authorities may be willing to conduct negotiations on behalf of a student.

If negotiations do not result in the settlement of a matter the second proce-dural aspect is the availability of the small claims jurisdictions. Whilst the precise names and jurisdictional limits (commonly AUD 5 000) vary from State to State or Territory, in each jurisdiction there is an informal process available for small claims. These processes emphasise in formal claims and personal presentation of cases without lawyers.

Responses of educational authorities

Fear of litigation can lead to overreaction. Already some educators have com-plained of pressures to pass students so as to retain their income for later years of a course. Complaints about quality can lead to similar responses – if students receive a pass they are going to have more difficulty establishing that the lack of quality has caused an identifiable and quantifiable loss. Education is not a product

135|

simply to be consumed rather students are provided with the relevant sources and skills to enable them to be able to perform.

For the issue of legal liability to arise, performance management must have broken down completely. It is unlikely to be a coincidence that complaints have been most common where association with the institution has been weakest. Legal liability only picks up crudest quality assurance breaches. It reinforces the need to be careful as to what is promised, and to keep information up to date and to monitor performance.

With respect to brochures and other course announcements the points that flow from the discussion to date are that whilst a disclaimer will not of itself be effective more discretionary language may be effective and statements relating to external qualifications require particular care. Often a list of subjects to be offered is subject to late change. The possibility of change must be expressed and not in small print. Contents of subjects should not be set out in dogmatic terms – "a subject may consider some of the following issues". This desirability of caution for legal reasons may run counter to educational objectives pointing to greater disclosure of content and aims.

The quality of a course cannot be assured simply by the reputation of the presenter. It is often said that the famous written lecture series only made it into print because as oral deliveries they were tough going. There is today less preparedness to sit at the feet of a great person and blame yourself if you cannot take in what is being delivered. Similarly today's audience has been used to entertainment from an early age.

If advertisers have any qualities they are that the advertiser depends on being able to capture attention. Educators similarly are becoming more and more expert on techniques for audience participation and appeal to all the senses.

To avoid complaint about the quality of a course an educational administrator thus has to have in place measures that impose standards whatever the shortcomings of any individual teacher. Standards for course outlines and materials, assessment guidelines, statements of course objectives and feedback on learning can be imposed. Procedures should be in place to disclose problems at any early stage – staff/student learning liaison teams and complaints procedures are part of the support for the teachers. All these steps have the benefit that as well as lessening the risks of legal liability they improve educational quality.

The Danish Parliamentary Omsudsman's Experience With Regard to the Legal Protection of Students

Jon Andersen

The Danish Parliamentary Ombudsman

The Danish Parliamentary Ombudsman Office was established in 1955 and was intended as an additional supervising body *vis-à-vis* the public administration. In practice the office has become more and more like an administrative court.

The Parliamentary Ombudsman is appointed by Parliament and he supervises all parts of the public administration on behalf of Parliament. The Ombudsman must be a law graduate and his assessment of public administration is primarily based on the legislation. However, the Ombudsman also evaluates decisions, behaviour, and procedures on the grounds of good administrative practice.

The Ombudsman can investigate individual cases as well as more general problems, either based on actual complaints or on his own initiative. However, the Ombudsman is not obliged to investigate a complaint. He may decide not to investigate a complaint and reject it even if the case lies within his jurisdiction, but such a rejection has, of course, to have legitimate grounds. The Ombudsman has jurisdiction over all public bodies except Parliament, institutions under Parliament, and the judiciary. His investigations are mostly directed towards institutions, not individual public servants. The main aim of an Ombudsman investigation is not to specify disciplinary sanctions against individual persons, but to assess technical aspects of a decision, a procedure, or a general enterprise, including whether or not it is lawful, whether it should be reassessed or amended, or whether it gives grounds for compensation.

When it comes to the investigation itself the Ombudsman has quite extensive powers. He can requisition all documents, files, and whatever kind of information he needs from the public administration. Rules of confidentiality or secrecy are no barriers in this connection. In practice even highly confidential matters from the intelligence services have been disclosed to the Ombudsman. He has the right to put all manner of questions to the administration, including those of an abstract or general nature. If need be, he can have public servants and politicians cross-examined in court.

The Ombudsman's supervisory powers are restricted in several ways. First of all, he cannot make binding decisions. He can state his point of view, he can criticize, he can recommend, or he can state that there has been no violation of the law. But he cannot annul, award damages, demand disciplinary sanctions, or make other kinds of binding decisions.

In many countries, for example in France, the Ombudsman is considered a mediator. In Denmark, the role of the Ombudsman Office is less that of a mediator and more like an administrative court. This is because the Danish Ombudsman's work is based almost exclusively on the legislation and his statements are based on legal grounds. General humanitarian values, what would be reasonable, what would be the best solution, or other such criteria do not enter into the assessment. The Ombudsman can only act if the public administration violates the law or the rules of good administrative practice.

In short, the office carries out traditional legal investigations.

This provides less scope for mediation than if the assessment had a broader content.

What type of cases are investigated?

At the moment the Ombudsman annually receives about 3 500-4 000 complaints, which concern all parts of the public administration. Most complaints stem from decisions made by the social administration, but the environmental authorities and the taxation administration also contribute considerably to the caseload, as do the immigration authorities.

In this respect, a comparatively small percentage of the complaints stems from the universities. University-level education is placed under a number of different ministries, among others the Ministry of Education, the Ministry of Information Technology and Research, and the Ministry of Food, Agriculture and Fisheries. An educated guess is that the Ombudsman investigates about 50 complaints annually from university-level students. Among others, the complaints concern state grants during the study period, examination and examination marks, recognition of foreign examination papers, public access to files at the higher educational facility, and the exclusion of students from the studies or the premises of the school. Other cases are lodged by teachers and researchers who have been turned down for positions as scholars, have had a thesis rejected, or have been sacked or transferred.

Two examples

Concrete examples are probably the best way of providing an impression of what the Ombudsman can accomplish in individual cases.

Example 1: the Ombudsman has recently processed a complaint from a student who did communication studies at one of our universities. He attended courses at an English university for one term. However, when he arrived at the English University it turned out that only a small part of the promised courses was available, so he had to make a change of plan. He communicated with some of his teachers at the Danish university via e-mail and got the impression that the courses he now chose to follow at the English university would be recognized as a substitute for a whole term at his own university. When he returned to Denmark he had difficulties in getting his examination certificate from the English university, which withheld them because the student was alleged to owe a private landlord about £50. The student asked for help but could not get any assistance from his Danish university to make the English university release the certificate. He received his certificate about one year later and by then the Danish university only recognized some of the courses he had taken, so he had to make a written report as well. All in all his studies were prolonged by 12 to 18 months.

The Ombudsman did not, of course, express any opinion as to whether the English communication courses should have been recognized from a professional point of view, but two legal points could be examined. Had the Danish university been sufficiently helpful? And were the e-mails sent by the Danish teachers legally binding for the university? As to the first question the Ombudsman expressed severe criticism. The passive attitude of the Danish university constituted a violation of the Danish *Public Administration* Act.

As for the second question, the Ombudsman did not find that the e-mails were legally binding decisions, but their content and wording could leave the student with the impression that his courses would be recognized. The Danish university and also the Ministry of Education should have taken this fact into consideration when they ruled on the merit transfer, but the Ombudsman did not – and could not – award the student damages for the delay of his studies.

Example 2: a seminary for a particular religious society complained that the Ministry of Education did not recognize its training, which meant that the students could not receive state grants during the studies. The Ombudsman did not criticize the decision, but examined very carefully whether the decision was in conflict with the protection of freedom of religion as stated in the Danish constitution or constituted a violation of the principle of equality. According to the Ombudsman this was not the case. On two points the Ombudsman criticized the Ministry of Education: the seminary should have been heard before the decision was made, and a reason for the decision should have been given.

To what extent are students' rights protected?

The Ombudsman can help students to get their legal rights as provided by the legislation. He himself does not formulate new legal provisions and does not interfere in individual cases where the grounds would be that a decision is unreasonable, uncivilized, and so forth.

Thus, the protection provided is highly dependent on the contents of the existing legal provisions. At least in Denmark, there is very little legislation that protects students against abuse of power.

As the first example shows, the lack of precise provisions concerning the recognition of merit transfers turned out to have great consequences for the student in question. It was decisive for the Ombudsman's investigation that the main issue, namely whether or not the student's English courses corresponded to courses taken at the Danish university, was dependent on the professional discretion of the university. The Danish university was criticized, but the student did not receive any compensation for his setbacks. This is, of course, due to the fact that the Danish Ombudsman exclusively reviews cases on the basis of the existing legislation and the fact that the legislation in this field is less precise.

The Danish Ombudsman has a part to play in cases like these but not as dominant a role as, for example, in cases concerning the rights of public servants against their employers or family law disputes.

Handling Student Grievances:
What Lessons are there for Institutions in the Cases
Brought before the Ombudsman in Australia?

Bruce Barbour

The relationship between ombudsman offices and universities in Australia

The first Parliamentary Ombudsman in Australia appeared in Western Australia in 1971. The office of the New South Wales (NSW) Ombudsman, was established in 1975, and by 1989, when the Australian Capital Territory became self-governing, every State and Territory had its own Ombudsman.

There seems to be a common misconception within the university community that universities are not actually part of the public sector. In part this arises from the fact that many universities receive most of their funding direct from the Federal Government.

However most universities are established by a State Act of Parliament, and as a result are accountable to the public, just like other State public sector bodies. Universities in NSW, for example, can be audited by the NSW Auditor-General and come within the jurisdiction of the NSW Ombudsman. The Ombudsman's role as a watchdog over universities is therefore an important aspect of our relationship.

But it is not the only role. Because people inevitably view their relationship with watchdogs with trepidation, it is important to understand that Ombudsman are primarily there to help not just complainants, as is commonly understood, but also those organisations that we oversee. Our aim is to promote fair decision-making and good conduct, which can really only be achieved if there is a co-operative relationship with those agencies.

All universities are accountable to those who fund their operations and to those who stand to benefit from the education and research the universities provide. Issues such as accountability, transparency, and fair processes are all the "bread and butter" work of the Ombudsman. Therefore at least some of the changes that universities are undergoing because of changing student expectations are matters in which the Ombudsman has considerable experience.

In 2000-01 my office dealt with nearly 10 000 written complaints and over 26 000 oral inquiries. Over 25 years, we have dealt with well over 100 000 written complaints. Our experience in dealing with complaints about maladministration is clearly extensive.

One significant lesson we have learned is that many complaints arise from poor communication by agencies. Sometimes there is a failure to communicate at all, and all too often otherwise simple inquiries escalate because they are not dealt with quickly and directly. By the time they reach our office, the complainant's irritation has been compounded by the way in which the agency has treated their original inquiry – sometimes by ignoring it.

I wish this were not the case, but some of the universities that we have dealt with recently have been equally prone to these problems.

We have also found that many problems with administration arise when policies are inadequate or non-existent. Staff who lack proper guidance often make decisions that are, although this is often unintended, unfair, discriminatory or improper.

However, having policies in place is not in itself a fail-safe method of ensuring proper decision-making. We recently conducted an investigation into a matter where a special consideration policy was repeatedly breached by several members of staff to increase the mark of an honours student by so much that in the end she was awarded first class honours.

One of the more serious breaches was when the student's mark was upgraded after, and apparently to some extent because, she burst into tears at a meeting with her examiners. This breached both the special consideration policy and another policy which stated that during such a meeting, the student's mark could only be upgraded if the student had performed well. We can safely assume this was intended to refer to the student's academic performance.

As this case demonstrates, our ability to investigate complaints can lead to significant outcomes. We uncovered serious deficiencies in the university's complaint processes, marking procedures and record-keeping practices.

In 2000-01 my office finalised 45 complaints about universities. Interestingly, most of these were received from academic members of staff. As well as breaches of policy, the complaints raised other serious issues, such as nepotism, conflict of interest, and failure to afford procedural fairness to an academic who was the subject of complaints. We have also heard of academics sitting on boards considering appeals from decisions that they had a part in making.

Most concerning has been the failure of some university staff, including those in senior management positions, to recognise these problems even after we have brought them to their attention.

Another important issue that we are finding universities slow to address is whistleblowing by employees. Our experience to date has been that many universities have not shown a willingness to support members of staff who criticise their operations. Students, in some ways, are in a similar position to whistleblowers, in that speaking up carries the risk of retribution.

There exists an inherent power imbalance between students and staff in all educational institutions. Students are there to receive an education. Staff provide that education and, importantly, are responsible for assessing how the student performs. The relationship lasts a number of years and it is not difficult to understand how a student would be particularly fearful of jeopardising their academic future by complaining.

In universities where the complaint handling mechanisms are not open and fair, students do not know where to turn in safety if they have concerns, making the student's position even more difficult.

If a student has a genuine grievance, they will not raise their concerns if they fear being punished or victimised for doing so. Real or perceived, this is an issue that must be dealt with directly. In one investigation, allegations from a number of students that their honours supervisor had sexually harassed them did not surface until after their final marks had been released. Sexual harassment is behaviour that no person should have to endure, but the students were scared that if they complained the supervisor would punish them through the marking system or by refusing to be involved in publishing their research work.

Universities need to develop strategies for protecting students from possible retribution by staff members who have been the subject of complaints. In an industrial environment where it is often difficult to take disciplinary proceedings against academics, we understand that this will be a challenge. But it is a challenge that cannot be avoided or ignored.

It is not unreasonable for a student to expect high standards of performance, academic and administrative, from a university. It is equally not unreasonable for the student to expect that their complaints and concerns will be taken seriously. Particularly in a climate where universities are charging more and more, and more students are footing the bill themselves, universities need to be more accountable than ever to their students.

Accountability does not require academic standards to be lowered. It does not mean that students' unreasonable expectations (such as, to take an extreme example, expecting to pass a course without having completed any of the assessment tasks) have to be fulfilled.

What accountability means is that processes need to be transparent. It means that students need to be told what to expect from university life, in particular, how

143

they are to be judged academically. And, more importantly, they must be judged in accordance with those standards.

Proper accountability means that information should be available to students, including policies about how the university makes decisions, such as assessing academic merit or providing financial support.

Universities throughout the country are already required to provide access to their records under Freedom of Information (FOI) legislation and most Ombudsmen play a role in ensuring that this legislation is complied with.

The experience in NSW has been that agencies across the board fail not only to comply with the technical requirements of our FOI Act, such as giving comprehensive reasons for refusing access, but also often act against the spirit of the Act.

I strongly encourage agencies to embrace values of transparency, not only because the public demands it and not only because transparency encourages better quality decision-making, but also because operating in a transparent way makes dealing with complaints much easier in the long run.

For example, when conducting the investigation into the honours student's mark, it was very difficult to find out exactly what had taken place, and how the student ended up with first class honours. Records of why certain decisions had been made had either not been written, or not been kept. The failure to record decisions properly does not simply prevent scrutiny of those decisions. This case clearly demonstrates that when problems with decisions finally surface, the lack of records also makes the problem much harder to resolve. In this case, the problems escalated, the university was taken to court, several times, and ended up with a legal bill of over USD 1 million.

Transparent practices, particularly good record-keeping, and a positive attitude towards providing access to those records, are essential for managing this risk.

The complaints received from students by Ombudsman in other States have raised concerns about various issues, including:

- Breaches of university ordinances and grievance procedures.
- Incompetent teaching.
- Failure to provide lectures and tutorials as represented in the course handbook.
- Refusal to return an assignment.
- Failure to provide adequate supervision.
- Incorrect marking of exam papers.

Some Ombudsmen have also seen an increasing tendency for students to complain to them about marks and assessment if they have not done as well as they expected.

The jurisdiction of Ombudsman over universities relates solely to matters involving maladministration. My focus is on ensuring that when students are being judged on their merit, the outcome of the process is fair and transparent. I do not consider it appropriate to involve myself in matters of academic merit.

The important thing to understand is that when students have concerns like "my mark is too low" or "the teacher was really bad" or "the course materials were not provided on time", the university itself is in the best position to deal with them. Complaints are usually an expression of dissatisfaction with the organisation or its staff. How do you reduce this dissatisfaction? A proper process for handling complaints is a good place to start.

This simple observation is one of the key issues that my office has identified from the many cases that we have handled.

The importance of a sound internal complaints system

Perhaps more than anyone else, my office understands that a proportion of complaints will be vexatious, frivolous, or raise issues that should not be our concern. A good complaints system, which allows you to establish institutional experience with complaints, helps to determine which complaints are legitimate and which are not.

These decisions in themselves must also be transparent and fair, and again, a good complaints system, with clear policies about what kind of complaint will be acted upon, and what kind of complaint will not be acted upon, provides that accountability.

Another important reason for having a good complaints system is that not having one can lead to an escalation of the complaint. The traditional approach of reacting defensively to criticism is not conducive to a quick resolution of a matter, and can lead to costly, drawn-out legal proceedings, potentially leaving everyone dissatisfied.

Put simply, most complaints involve a person who has a grievance, and a person who is the subject of the grievance. To deal with the grievance properly, the university must not take sides. It must be impartial, otherwise the whole process is tainted and unfair from the outset. Reacting defensively is in effect taking the side of the person who is the subject of the grievance.

Automatically taking the side of the student with the grievance can be just as a big a minefield. That is exactly what happened with the investigation into the sexual harassment allegations referred to earlier. The academic who was the subject of the allegations took the university to court and in its judgement, the court specifically criticised the university for having taken the students' side from the beginning, and treating the academic as an adversary. The academic was not

145|

afforded procedural fairness and, in the end, the investigation was so flawed that even the students concerned were not satisfied.

Another important reason why an internal complaints system is so important is that complaints should be viewed as a form of feedback on performance. Any well-managed organisation needs to address firstly the immediate concerns of the complainant, and secondly any issues of a systemic nature that the complaint raises. A good complaints system will aim to address the complainant's specific grievance and provide a good starting point for fixing any underlying problems.

Having a good complaints system is one thing, but it will not be effective unless people actually know about it, and feel comfortable using it. My office actively encourages organisations to educate their staff and customers about their complaints system. The problem with organisations where complaining is frowned upon – where "rocking the boat" is not the done thing – is that people with genuine grievances will not air them. Everybody loses. University management loses the opportunity to improve its processes and the person with the grievance does not have it resolved.

In June 2001, an Australian newspaper editorial said about university vice-chancellors:

"As heads of income-generating organisations, their roles are more complex and they are accountable, financially and morally, to a larger range of groups than before…Proper governance has always been at the heart of a university's success. Like their corporate counterparts, good governing boards should take an active role in ensuring accountability, monitoring academic standards, formulating strategic policy and assessing the performance of vice-chancellors and other executives" (The Australian, 12 June 2001, p. 14).

Undoubtedly, some universities are showing a better understanding of these issues. I am encouraged by the number of universities around the country that have established Student Ombudsman positions, or are in the process of establishing them.

Complaints should be seen as a rich source of information. My office has consistently found that if collected and analysed properly, complaints can help management identify problems in areas such as procedure, staffing and administration.

The experiences of my office also suggest other strategies that can be used to reduce student dissatisfaction.

Students, just like customers, become dissatisfied when their expectations do not correlate with the reality of their experience.

For many years now, both State and Commonwealth public sector agencies have been required to have guarantees of service and performance standards in place. It is important to make sure that the standards are linked to what consumers think is important and that they be realistic.

Each year my office conducts what we call "mystery shopper" programs to test these standards in a few select organisations. Members of my staff pose as consumers and provide to the organisation feedback about timeliness, the accuracy of information provided, and the quality of their customer service. It is a pure "put yourself in the other person's shoes" approach.

This kind of methodology may be useful to universities, to understand generally what students actually expect, and to understand better what the organisation is delivering and what it is able to deliver.

Student expectations vary, and realistically a university is never going to be able to fulfil the expectations of each and every student. However, it is still important that universities clearly communicate to students what they can expect from particular courses and from other aspects of university life. It is understandable that universities would be tempted to paint a rosy picture for potential students in order to market their services effectively. However, the problem is that this kind of marketing can create false expectations which the university cannot later meet.

One example is the expectations that students have about how hard you have to work to get through a degree. If students do not understand fully, and young people often do not, that their money is paying for educational services, and not a degree, there is a risk that they may become dissatisfied if they do not do well.

Universities therefore have the capacity to influence both student expectations as well as their experiences, by ensuring that the university is performing to a high standard in the way they educate, evaluate and otherwise support their students in their academic studies.

These strategies, properly supported by a good complaints system, should help to reduce student dissatisfaction.

Characteristics of a good complaints system

First, the organisation, and particularly senior management, must have a good attitude to complaints. There must be a high level of commitment to a fair and open process. Complaints must be welcomed to prevent them.

Part of having a good attitude is recognising that the university as a whole must take responsibility for a student's dissatisfaction, and that blaming either the complainant or an individual staff member is often inappropriate.

Second, the system must be simple and accessible. The process for lodging and dealing with complaints must be user-friendly: it must be easy to understand. The people primarily using the system will be the complainant and the staff members processing the complaint, and it must be accessible to both.

Third, the system must be clear. That is, the responsibilities and rights of each person who is involved in a complaint – the student, any member of staff who is the subject of the complaint, and the members of staff dealing with the complaint – must be clear. They all have to know clearly what to expect and what not to expect from the process. For example, the student should be given advice about alternative remedies or avenues of redress so that they can be fully informed of their options.

Fourth, the system must be sufficiently flexible, so that special cases can be dealt with, and it is clear who is responsible for dealing with them. The most appropriate method for resolving a complaint should also be used, for example some complaints could be best resolved through quick, alternative dispute resolution processes such as mediation.

Fifth, the system must provide appropriate and reasonable remedies. In doing so, the system must be fair and impartial. What this means is that the system needs to have the capacity to take into account not only the concerns of the student complaining, and not only the concerns of the staff member who is the subject of the complaint, but also other factors such as whether or not a particular remedy would be fair to other students. One example where this would be an issue is where a student complains that his or her mark is too low.

It is very important that any investigation afford procedural fairness to anyone who is the subject of the complaint. It is also important to remember that even if students are viewed as "customers", this does not mean that the "customer" is always right. What it does require is a recognition that the student and the university have a continuing relationship, and the university has an interest in making this relationship as positive as possible. Given that there are increasing numbers of students undertaking second degrees and higher qualifications, this relationship has the potential to last quite a number of years.

The system must also provide for information to be recorded. This will allow the information to be analysed so that management can assess the damage suffered as a result of dissatisfaction with the university, and develop an informed response. This may include improving processes, undertaking disciplinary action or providing clearer information to students about what to expect from a course, from an activity, or from a service – at the beginning of their university experience. It will also prevent inaccurate, negative perceptions from developing.

Keeping proper records is also good administrative practice and allows the university to assess the performance of the complaints system itself.

Finally, and this may actually be one of the more important elements of a good complaints system, the system must be adequately resourced. Staff must be supported and properly trained in complaint-handling techniques.

In recognising this, my office has been active in providing guidelines for establishing proper complaints systems across the state.

In addition to these points, universities must keep in mind that the system will not work unless the long-held fears of students are allayed. Students should be reassured that their complaints will be taken seriously and that they can expect a result, even if it is simply providing a better explanation of what has caused the complaint. At the end of the complaints process, comprehensive feedback should be provided to students so that they are kept properly informed and their confidence in the system preserved.

Finally, as noted earlier, it is essential that students be protected from retribution for coming forward.

Conclusion

At a conference in 2000 on university governance, the then NSW Education Minister, Mr. Aquilina said:

"Universities have a legislative responsibility for fulfilling a teaching and research mandate. University councils have a legislative responsibility for overseeing the implementation of that mandate."

His emphasis on the proper management of universities from within is exactly the point I have been making. External scrutiny is still important, but it is better for an Ombudsman to have a co-operative relationship with universities and to take a co-ordinated approach to solving problems. This may have been the thinking behind a proposal by the then Minister to require universities to report publicly each year on how they were implementing Ombudsman recommendations.

Universities must themselves establish sound internal systems. The most effective way to deal with student grievances is not to run away from them, but to tackle them head on. An open and direct approach to complaints is better than having complaints dealt with by an external third party such as a University Ombudsman. Ombudsmen have considerable experience and expertise in dealing with complaints. Fostering a co-operative relationship with Ombudsman will allow universities to draw on this experience to improve the way their students' grievances are handled.

Notes on Authors

Jon Andersen is Deputy Permanent Secretary in the Office of the Parliamentary Commissioner for Civil and Military Administration (Folketingets Ombudsmand) in Copenhagen, Denmark (*www.ombudsmanden.dk/*).

Bruce Barbour is the Ombudsman for the State of New South Wales, Australia (*www.nswombudsman.nsw.gov.au/*).

Jarmila Bastova is researcher at the Centre for Higher Education Studies in the Ministry for Education, Youth and Sports in the Czech Republic.

John Byron was President during 2001 of the Council of Australian Postgraduate Associations, the peak body representing Australia's postgraduate students at the national level(*www.capa.edu.au*).

Peter Coaldrake is Deputy Vice-Chancellor of Queensland University of Technology in Brisbane, Australia (*www.qut.edu.au*).

Michael Conlon is Director of Research for the Canadian Federation of Students (*www.cfs-fcee.ca*).

Sarah Davies is Vice-President, External Affairs, at Swinburne University in Victoria, Australia (*www.swin.edu.au/corporate/marketing/external.htm*).

Ruth Dunkin is Vice-Chancellor and President of RMIT University in Melbourne, Australia (*www.rmit.edu.au*).

Dennis Farrington was Deputy Secretary of Stirling University in Scotland. In 2002 he took up the post of Secretary-General of the SEE University in Tetovo, Macedonia (*www.see-university.com*).

Michael Gallagher is Group Manager of the International Group within the Department of Education, Science and Training (formerly Education, Training and Youth Affairs) in Australia (*www.dest.gov.au/highered/*).

Richard James is an Associate Professor in the Centre for the Study of Higher Education at the University of Melbourne, Australia (*www.cshe.unimelb.edu.au*).

Anthony P. Moore is Associate Professor of Law at Flinders University in South Australia (*wwwehlt.flinders.edu.au/law/staff/tony_moore.html*).

Eva Münsterova is Vice-President, Brno University of Technology, the Czech Republic (*www.fme.vutbr.cz/*).

Ales Vlk is a PhD candidate at CHEPS, the University of Twente, the Netherlands.

OECD PUBLICATIONS, 2, rue André-Pascal, 75775 PARIS CEDEX 16
PRINTED IN FRANCE
(89 2002 04 1 P) ISBN 92-64-19824-5 – No. 52589 2002